AN IRISHMAN LOOKS AT
HIS WORLD

AN IRISHMAN LOOKS
AT HIS WORLD

914.15
B

BY
GEORGE A. BIRMINGHAM
Author of "General John Regan," "Benedict Kavanah," &c.

pseud

HODDER AND STOUGHTON
LONDON   NEW YORK   TORONTO
MCMXIX

CONTENTS

CHAPTER I

CHAPTER II

CHAPTER III

CHAPTER IV

CHAPTER V

CONTENTS

CHAPTER VI

CHAPTER VII

CHAPTER VIII

CHAPTER IX

CHAPTER X

CHAPTER XI

CHAPTER XII

AN IRISHMAN LOOKS AT HIS WORLD

CHAPTER I

IRISH POLITICS—THE OLD PARTIES

THE most striking feature of Irish politics is the stability of parties.

Here Ireland differs from England, and indeed from every other country where people possess voting power. Elsewhere one party succeeds another in popular favour, and any party may hope to win a majority at the polls. The voters transfer their allegiance, change their opinions, and there is always a chance of persuading them by speeches, posters, newspaper articles, and personal solicitation to support a cause which a little whil before they hated. In Ireland no such thing is possible. The Nationalist remains steadfastly Nationalist. The Unionist remains steadfastly Unionist. No one imagines that the opinions of the voter can be altered by any means.

It is true that the last General Election saw the complete defeat of a great Parliamentary party, a defeat which amounted to annihilation and is unparalleled in English election history. But though the change was great, it was something quite different from the change that takes place when the Conservative Party wins a victory over the Liberal Party in an English election. We passed through a political revolution, but every Nationalist constituency still elected a Nationalist, and every Unionist constituency still elected a Unionist. The new kind of Nationalist was just as impotent in Unionist Ulster as his predecessors of the old party had been. No Unionist, in spite of the sudden dissolution of party loyalty, stood the smallest chance of winning a

10

seat in Nationalist Ireland. There were startling changes, but essentially the old stability remained. Nationalist Ireland altered its tactics, not its aim. Unionist Ireland altered nothing. As between Nationalist and Unionist there was no change at all. No body of voters large enough to be discernible in the election returns passed from one side to the other.

This stability makes Irish politics a simple business. It has for a long time been possible to say beforehand with certainty what the strength of each party will be after a General Election. There is a very small margin of possible change, two or three constituencies which are doubtful. But even in them an election is not fought, as elections are in England, with speeches, arguments and accusations calculated to influence dubious voters. In Ireland there are no dubious voters. The elections in the doubtful constituencies are really fought and won or lost months beforehand in the courts of the revising barristers. The question for the party leaders is not how to persuade a few uncertain men to vote for a particular candidate, but how to get votes for those who are sure to support one candidate and how to exclude from the register those who are sure to support the other.

This stability has certain advantages, but it has one disastrous effect. Since it is plainly useless to try to persuade anyone to vote against his party, there is no public discussion of political questions. Our candidates make speeches, of course, but they never make speeches intended to convince their opponents. They speak only to their supporters, being comfortably aware that no one except their supporters will listen to them or afterwards read what they say. So, since it is foolish to bring forward arguments to convince those convinced before, a political speaker in Ireland has nothing to do except to shout ancient phrases and devise new forms of abuse. No effort is ever made by men of either party to state their case to their opponents. The ordinary Nationalist voter does not know that there is anything to be said for the Union. For him a Unionist is simply an obstinately wicked man whose ways are as incomprehensible as they are detestable. The ordinary Unionist does not know, because he has never heard, what the Nationalist has to say for himself. For him the political issue is a simple matter of keeping blackguards from obtaining power. Questions of Irish policy are no doubt argued out and cases stated in important and expensive magazines. But the ordinary voter does not read important and expensive magazines. He depends for guidance on speeches and articles in small papers. He gets no argument or discussion in either the one or the other. Intimate friends, if they happen to be educated men, will occasionally discuss politics with each other. But the ordinary Irishman does not discuss politics with his neighbour. It is a gross breach of good manners to suggest that a man's political faith is wrong. It would scarcely be more offensive to tell him that his wife's

13

virtue is doubtful. He is bound to believe in his politics and his wife's honour. He would, very naturally, resent an attempt to discuss either.

Irish politics have been stable for so long that we are apt to forget that they ever were anything else, and find it very difficult to believe that they can ever become fluid. Yet half a century ago there was no solid Nationalist Ireland and no unchanging Unionist Ulster. Also it is possible, even now, to discern signs of the existence of a new force in Irish politics which may cut slantways across both the old divisions.

It is an interesting and curious thought that our present stability followed the enfranchisement of the voter. Political theorists sometimes assert that democracy is essentially changeable, that a crowd is never long of the same mind. In Ireland experience leads us to the opposite opinion. During the first three quarters of the nineteenth century, while the franchise slowly widened, the Irish voter remained in leading strings. He voted as he was bidden, sometimes as he was bidden by his landlord, sometimes as he was bidden by his priest, with a fear constantly present in his mind of material loss or spiritual disaster. He did not vote according to his own wishes or opinions. While he was thus shepherded he was unstable, and Irish constituencies both in the north and south might change and did change from one party to another. Elections were contested, in the same sense in which elections are contested in England. There was no certainty about the results of Irish elections then. Candidates argued, schemed and threatened, when they could, with a view to obtain votes, for voters could be influenced. It was possible to detach a body of voters from one party and to swing them over to the support of another. During the last quarter of the nineteenth century the Irish voter broke his leading reins, became a free man and voted as he chose, not as he was told. He ranged himself at once; became Nationalist or

Unionist; and Nationalist or Unionist he has remained ever since, unwavering. The beginning of democratic freedom—whatever it may have been elsewhere—has in Ireland been the beginning of political steadfastness.

I. The Irish Nationalists, in spite of the faithfulness of the people at the polls and in spite of an almost perfect party discipline, have never possessed a fundamental unity. There have always been two parties, and the first problem of the leaders has been to keep the two parties together so as to present an unbroken front to the Unionist enemy. We distinguish between moderate and extreme Nationalists, sometimes between constitutional agitators and believers in physical force. In reality the division is something quite other than the difference between the moderate man and the extremist, who generally agree about their point of departure and only fall out over the question of how far to go. Nor can we be satisfied with classing Irish Nationalists as con-

16

stitutional or advocates of physical force.
No one would advocate an appeal to arms—
in Ireland's case a singularly hopeless
venture—if he saw any other way of
getting what he wanted. No one would
continue to use constitutional means,
merely for the sake of being constitutional,
if he were quite convinced that they
offered no chance of attaining his end.
The most vehement advocate of physical
force would prefer a peaceful argument
if he thought it any use. Few would be
found to deny the abstract proposition
that an appeal to force may sometimes be
right.

The difference between the two sections
of Nationalists is deeper down. It lies
in their reason for being Nationalists.
There are Nationalists who believe that
the union between England and Ireland
ought to be dissolved because it works
badly or does not work at all; perhaps
because it works to the disadvantage of
Ireland. This is the position of a practical
man who sees things as they are, who

17   c

wants to arrive at the best arrangement he can for Ireland, the country he belongs to ; perhaps also for the Empire of which he may reckon himself a citizen. This man has a very great deal to say for himself. He can appeal to the fact that England is and must be the predominant partner in any union between the two countries and will consider her own interests first. He can maintain, quite rightly, that the life of England is so different from the life of Ireland that the interests of the two countries are seldom or never identical. He can produce instances of laws which suit England and do not suit Ireland, which nevertheless Ireland must accept, at great inconvenience. He can assert, without much fear of contradiction, that the Union, which is now more than a hundred years in existence, has not been a success, that Ireland is profoundly dissatisfied, that England is perpetually irritated by a sore in the body politic. So much and a great deal more this Nationalist can say in justification

18

of his demand for some measure of Home Rule, for Colonial Independence, for the complete independence of an Irish Republic. He may see hope in the most moderate measure of self-government or no hope without absolute separation. He may be an extremist or he may be a moderate; but he is a Nationalist of expediency, a pragmatist in politics. He wants what will work best and would secure the fullest possible good for his country. If the Union worked well he might be and should be a Unionist.

There are also Nationalists who believe that Ireland is a distinct nation and therefore entitled to a separate existence. This is the position of the idealist, who sees things not precisely as they are but as they must be. He demands for his country an inalienable and indisputable right. He, too, has much to say for himself. He points to the fact that Ireland once had a civilisation of her own, a language of her own, her own system of jurisprudence; that Ireland has never consented to be

19   c 2

anglicised; that though centuries have passed since the Brehon Laws ruled the lives of Irishmen and Gaelic culture flourished in Irish schools, yet Irishmen have never developed a loyalty to English law or a love of English civilisation. He may assert, again without much fear of contradiction, that Ireland remains to-day as different from England in mind, in spirit, in all essential things, as she was before Strongbow married the Princess Eva.

It is seldom possible to disentangle one kind of Nationalism from the other. They have always been mixed together, and the public utterances of Nationalist leaders suggest that they consider it desirable in the interest of their party and their cause to avoid clear thought and precise definition. Yet it is plain that the difference is of the utmost importance to those who must deal with what is called the Irish problem. If the majority of Irish Nationalists are of the first kind, then the policy of the English Conservatives—or perhaps we should say the declared policy of the

20

English Conservatives—has a fair chance of success. If every Irish grievance were removed, if in every respect Ireland had fair play, if the country became materially prosperous, if its economic problems were justly settled, the Nationalism of expediency and convenience would cease to exist. There would be no reason for its existence. Englishmen of good will, conscious of having done their best for Ireland and still wishing to do their best, are puzzled by the continued existence of irreconcilable Nationalism. They do not understand that a policy of reform and amelioration and the granting of every reasonable demand do not affect the position of the idealist. To him anything that tends to make Ireland content with the Union is of the nature of a bribe. All that is best in him rises up in protest against the doctrine that it can profit a nation to gain the whole world, if in gaining it she lose her own soul.

It is because of this difference between Nationalists that their leaders have never been able to say precisely what they want, or to give a pledge that this or that measure will be accepted as a final settlement. It is extremely difficult to say that any measure of Home Rule would remove all the practical grievances of Ireland. It is utterly impossible to say that a nation, driven by the very law of its being to seek self-expression, will find the desired opportunity under any constitution short of actual independence. The plain man has asked the Irish leaders what they want, has asked impatiently, and has been angry when he got no answer. He does not realise that no Irish leader can answer that question; not merely because his political position forces him to be ambiguous, lest he lose the support of one section or another of his followers, but because the question is in itself unanswerable. Parnell understood that when he said " No man can set bounds to the march of a nation."

The Irish Party in Parliament came into existence under Isaac Butt. There had, of course, been Irishmen in Parliament

before his time who devoted themselves to
the interests of Ireland, men like George
Henry Moore. But Butt was the first
leader of a distinct Nationalist Party.
He was a lawyer and believed in the
possibility of persuading men by argument.
He failed to persuade Englishmen of any
party that Home Rule for Ireland was
desirable. It is the fashion in Ireland now
to condemn Butt as a weakling. But
there is something to be said for his policy.
No one in his time understood the true
nature of a modern Parliament. The
House of Commons was still regarded as a
deliberative assembly in which men con-
sulted together, listened to argument, and
made up their minds how to act. We
know now that a Parliament is nothing of
the sort, that it is an assembly of delegates,
each bound to vote with his party whatever
the right or wrong of any question may
be. The party leader, or the "boss" behind
the leader, is autocratic and supreme. It
is plainly useless to argue for the benefit
of delegates, who are mere recorders of

votes. The delegate's reason and his
opinion have nothing whatever to do with
the way his vote is cast. But to Isaac
Butt and his friends this was not obvious.
They believed that votes in Parliament
followed personal conviction. Perhaps in
those days they still actually did. The
policy of trying to convince seemed to be,
and was, a reasonable one.

Parnell tried another policy, the policy
of the high hand. Instead of persuading
he bullied. He aimed at degrading Parliament and making the conduct of public
business impossible until his demands were
granted. Parliament replied to his obstruction by altering its rules of procedure
in such a way that naked obstruction
became impossible. Parnell altered his
tactics and threatened, not Parliament
itself, but the leaders and " bosses " of
English political parties. He was strong
enough in any ordinary Parliament to
make it impossible for either party to take
its legitimate turn at governing. He said
in effect to the leaders of both parties,

" You must give me what I want or I shall prevent your holding office." Parnell came very near success. He was beaten because the English party leaders preferred coalition to submission. Men of parties violently opposed to each other shook hands and so became strong enough to hold office in spite of Parnell.

Redmond, who succeeded Parnell, tried a third policy. He entered into an informal alliance with one of the two English parties. He pledged it to grant his demands. He agreed to fight by its side in opposition and to support it when in power. He kept his part of the bargain faithfully. The English Liberals, after much hesitation, tried to keep theirs. They did not do so completely, perhaps they could not, and Redmond, like Butt and Parnell, failed.

Then came the election which ended, for a time at least, the existence of an Irish Party in Parliament. Irish Nationalists, having repudiated Butt's policy of persuasion and refused to follow out Parnell's policy of bullying, perceived the failure of Redmond's policy of alliance. There does not seem to be any other possible policy for a Parliamentary leader, and so Parliamentary action, though not necessarily constitutional action, came to be regarded in Ireland as useless. It had been tried and found wanting.

Irish Nationalism remained unchanged. Nationalists of expediency still chafed under what they felt to be an unwise and irritating kind of government. Nationalists of idealism still clung to their passionate belief in the rights of an Irish nation. The two kinds of Nationalists are still in alliance, still for the most part think and feel confusedly, still use one another's arguments without consciousness of any inconsistency. But both are convinced of the futility of Parliamentary action. Both have cast about for some new way of winning what they desire.

II. Irish Unionism is divided geographically. The Unionists of North-East Ulster form a powerful party. The Unionists of the rest of Ireland are almost impotent.

At the last election they won only one seat
—leaving out of the count Dublin University, a peculiar constituency whose electors
are not necessarily Southern Irishmen.
But these Unionists are not wholly without
political power. Their party commands
respect. It contains men of ability and
character whose opinions can scarcely be
ignored even in Ireland. It possesses
influence, if not voting power, in the
councils of the State, and it has shown that
it is not irreconcilable. Unlike the Bour-
bons, the Southern Irish Unionist is capable
of forgetting and of learning—of forgetting
the old story of the agrarian struggle with its
hatred and crimes and learning that Irish
Nationalism is something other, or at least
might be something other, than a class
struggle, soiled with religious jealousy. The
real weakness of the Southern Unionists lies
in the fact that they are in effect a party of
gentlemen, and gentlemen are not much
use in politics, just as D'Artagnan with his
rapier and his code of fighting honour
would not be much use in a modern

bayonet charge, however gallant and debonair he showed himself.

The Ulster Party, understanding the weakness of Unionism outside Ulster, and failing to appreciate the moral value of the old unity, has deserted the Southern Unionists. In justifying their action they will perhaps quote the prophet Isaiah, for the Ulsterman likes to feel that he has the support of the Bible. "They were all ashamed of a people that could not profit them, nor be a help nor a profit, but a shame and also a reproach." That must be very much the way the Belfast democracy feels about the Southern Unionists, even though these impotent folk are still in a position to send princes to Zoan and ambassadors to Hanes.

The Ulster Unionists are strong, astonishingly strong. Though a minority, and a small minority, in Ireland, they have succeeded up to the present moment in imposing their will upon the rest of the country. The legal Union between Ireland and England remains a fact. The rest of Ireland made its mind up long ago. The majority of Englishmen and Scotsmen decided lately that the Union must be dissolved.

North-East Ulster said " No," and North-East Ulster prevailed. The fact requires some explanation. We are supposed to be a democracy, and the one clear principle of democracies is that the will of the majority must prevail. Yet in this single case the will of the majority has not prevailed. Since the struggle began there has been a steady majority in Ireland in favour of a dissolution of the Union, more or less complete. There has several times been a large majority in Parliament in favour of some form of Home Rule. The minority in Ireland is small, so small that it might be regarded as helpless. Yet it has shown itself, so far, the stronger party.

A minority, led by men of conspicuous ability, can sometimes in a modern State hold a majority at bay by clever tactics, astute political moves, and a policy of insinuating divisions among its opponents. But the Ulster Unionist Party has never had leaders of conspicuous ability. It has produced no Parnell, no Gladstone. Its political action has never been clever or its tactics astute. It might on several occasions have taken advantage of divisions in Nationalist Ireland. It had not, apparently, sufficient intelligence to do so. I remember discussing the position of the Ulster Party with a Northern Unionist just after the introduction of the last Home Rule Bill. He deplored the stupidity—the word was his, not mine—of his friends. " If such a one "—he named a leading Ulster Unionist—" were to die to-morrow and to be buried, the whole brains of Ulster Unionism would lie in that grave." The statement was an exaggeration, though not a very grave one. Later on, in 1913, when the Ulster Volunteer movement had caught public attention, I listened one day to a discussion. " Is Ulster in earnest," some one asked, " or is it putting up a great bluff ? " A very able man, much experienced in political affairs and international diplomacy, closed the discussion with a definite pronouncement, " Ulster must be in earnest. She is too stupid to bluff." This, too, was an exaggeration. But it remains indisputably true that North-East Ulster has not displayed striking political ability or the faculty for manipulating events to her own advantage. Yet North-East Ulster has prevailed. The blank " We'll not have it " of Belfast has torn through the spider webs of politicians and rendered the voting powers of majorities impotent.

Nationalist Ireland might be wise, even now, to paint her cheeks, tire her hair, to don the soft garments of Delilah, to take the head of this blundering Samson on her lap and whisper to him : " Tell me, I pray thee, where thy great strength lieth and wherewith thou mightest be bound to afflict thee." After a while, having tried the green withes and the new cart ropes, she might learn the secret and shear the invincible locks.

31

No doubt great strength lies in the fact that Ulster is plainly and simply in earnest. The Northern Unionist has not, for many years now, regarded politics as a game, played by rules, in which each player does his best to win, but if he loses, still abiding by the rules, either scowls or smiles and pays. Ulster is content to let the cards be dealt, to sort her hand, to make her declaration; but when her opponent unexpectedly leads an ace which must capture the decisive trick, she throws down her hand and threatens to upset the table, cards and all. The ordinary player, the English politician, trained to the game and unable to realise that there are people in the world who are not playing games, stands aghast, bewildered, and passes into a state of speechless indignation. Then, foaming a little at the mouth, he picks up his ace again. Nationalist Ireland, which is also in earnest, has rapidly grasped the fact that it is possible for both sides to kick the table over. She has learned something, but not yet the whole secret of where the great strength lies. Mere refusal to obey is useless unless behind the refusal there is some power to make the refusal good. The ladies who swore they would not soil their tongues by licking gummy stamps did not indefinitely hang up the National Insurance Act. Ulster did hang up the Home Rule Act, though it stood in seeming safety, the law of this realm, on the pages of the Statute-book. The secret of the great strength is still to seek.

Ulster Unionism is itself a union, and a union of forces so naturally opposed to each other that even a temporary alliance between them might well seem impossible. In North-East Ulster only does the Irish aristocracy, the nobility and landed gentry, still hold political power. Ulster has admitted its aristocracy to leadership and gained strength thereby. For the Irish aristocracy has a traditional knowledge of great affairs and a hereditary ability in leading. Its members take a place among the great of the Empire. Its elders

are present in secret council chambers.
Its sons are not afraid of fighting. Soldiers
know them and count them kin. In the
last resort, when armed forces face each
other, men are unwilling to draw their
swords against their kin. And this class
in Ulster, as everywhere in Ireland, is
Unionist by strong conviction. It regards
the Union as a bulwark for the safety of the
Empire. Nationalism in Ireland appears
as a disruptive force, disloyal, dangerous.
This aristocracy is not greatly moved by
the fears for religion which are a force in
Ulster Unionism. Nor is it deeply concerned with the dread of incompetent
financial management which affects a business city like Belfast. But it is filled with
the imperial spirit and is conscious of fine
imperial pride. This is small wonder, since
for centuries it has taken a great part in
building up the Empire. Its knowledge of
the world is wide enough to enable it to
realise how good a thing it is to claim
citizenship in the mightiest State on earth.
It is satisfying to see flying over tropical

palm and northern pine and over every sea in all the world the flag; and to say "My fathers carried it forth. My sons fight for it." Convinced, not altogether without reason, that Nationalist Ireland hates the flag and wishes to destroy the Empire, this aristocracy will agree to no weakening of the Union.

Alongside the aristocracy, in the front rank of Ulster Unionism, are the business men and manufacturers of Belfast. The alliance seems an unnatural one, for these two classes are not usually sympathetic. Perhaps nothing but a common danger could have joined them together in the north of Ireland. Danger, like misfortune, makes strange bedfellows. Yet, while both dread Nationalism and any weakening of the Union, they have different reasons for their fear. Belfast's captains of industry are no doubt imperialists, believing that trade follows the flag. But they care for their trade more than they love the flag, or perhaps they love the flag chiefly because trade follows it. Their fear is that in submitting to the rule of Irish Nationalists they would submit to the rule of men who are incompetent, who would muddle the finance of the country in such a way that the prosperity of Ulster's business would be in danger. Sometimes their fear is more definite still and has a sharper edge to it. The rest of Ireland is, so they think, not only incompetent. It is lazy and greedy. Belfast under a Home Rule Parliament would be the milch cow of the rest of Ireland, and Belfast would be milked dry. On all promises and assurances of security, on all fair-sounding professions of brotherly love, Belfast's commercial men look slantways with cold, distrustful eyes. They say, with perfect truth, that they have done well under the Union, have been free to grow and prosper. They argue, with fair show of reason, that the rest of Ireland might have done well under the Union too, if it were capable of doing well at all or prospering. If not—if, as they believe the rest of Ireland is corrupt, extravagant and idle—then to be placed under the power

of the rest of Ireland would be intolerable.
And any way, " We won't be governed by
a Parliament in Dublin." Is not the
reputation of the Dublin Corporation
reason enough for such a decision ?

But an aristocracy is nowadays a feeble
thing, and a Chamber of Commerce, though
stronger, is not very strong. Not even
the union of the territorial aristocracy with
the captains of industry would be able to
resist the rest of Ireland if there were not a
third member of the alliance, the Northern
Protestant working man. He, for his
own peculiar reason, hates the idea of
Home Rule so much that he is content to
follow the leadership, and in matters
purely political to do the bidding, of those
whom working men elsewhere regard as the
enemies of their class. His obedience is
no evidence of a servile spirit. There is
not anywhere to be found a working man
more aggressively independent, more
radical, than the Belfast artisan. He
follows leaders and submits to discipline
because he is mastered by a fear which is

stronger than his class consciousness. He is not, any more than any other working man, passionately enamoured of the imperial idea. He cannot be supposed to be ready to fight in order to save his masters, the merchants and manufacturers, from having to pay an excessive income tax. He dreads the dissolution of the Union because he believes that the Pope would govern a Home-ruled Ireland. The root of his Unionism is religion, not so much attachment to one faith as fear of the domination of another.

It must not be supposed that these divisions of Ulster Unionism are clear-cut or that the motive, the fear, which animates each class is pure and unmixed. Things are never so simple as that in life. The religious feeling, the acute, explosive Protestantism of North-East Ulster, is present in all classes, colouring the imperialism of the aristocracy, spiritualising the business instincts of the manufacturers. The dread of financial incompetence and unfair dealing exists in all classes, and there is, throughout the whole Ulster Unionist Party, a certain imperial loyalty. But, in spite of apparent confusion, the three fears are separable. The strength of the Unionism of North-East Ulster lies in the fact that it has welded three divergent and naturally antipathetic classes into one party. It is a party which more than any other party represents a whole community, all classes of it. It is a party which for the sake of a common cause is content, and glad, at times of danger to forget all jealousies and sink all differences. Therefore beyond other parties it is strong.

The most hopeless feature of the political situation in Ireland is that neither party has any plan at all for dealing with its opponents, except one—force. Up to a certain point both Nationalist and Unionist appear to believe in conciliation. Ulster —every Nationalist has said it over and over again—will be given every safeguard, every guarantee consistent with the integrity of Ireland. Ireland—has not every Unionist said it ?—must have every fair play, every concession, every chance, all she asks, consistent with the maintenance of the Union, at least for North-East Ulster. But if Unionist Ulster will not even say what guarantees she wants— but if Nationalist Ireland will not be satisfied with any reasonable concessions, then there is nothing for it but firm government; the firm government of a Dublin Parliament, or of Dublin Castle. In the end it comes to this : " If the others won't agree with us—and we are most reasonable, quite easy to get on with and full of good intentions—then the others must submit, must be made to submit." No one, not even the peacemakers of our shadowy middle parties, not even our most moderate and conciliatory men, have anything to say in the end except that. No one has suggested any other way out of the bog in which we flounder.

Perhaps there is no other way.

Yet it is possible to hope. The hand which holds the kaleidoscope in which men's affairs fall into their patterns turns the tube. The fragments of coloured glass are shaken and moved. They slip past one another, dropping into fresh places. The star shapes, the ribbons and squares on which our eyes rested dissolve, and new combinations are formed, unexpected, startling. "Things must be thus or thus," says the logician; "nothing else is possible." God smiles. Events march on, and things are neither thus nor thus. Perhaps even now in this valley of dry bones there is a movement, "a noise and behold a shaking."

CHAPTER II

IRISH POLITICS—THE NEW PARTIES

In 1899 Mr. Arthur Griffith established
in Dublin a weekly paper called *The
United Irishman*. In 1904 he published
in it a series of articles on the struggle of
the Hungarian Magyars for political independence. He republished the articles
as a pamphlet under the title " The
Resurrection of Hungary." He suggested
that Ireland might and should adopt a
similar policy.

His pamphlet appeared at a time of
profound political apathy. Parnell's
policy of bullying the leaders of the
English parties had been abandoned. Redmond's policy of alliance with the Liberals
had not declared itself. The Nationalist
leaders were squabbling with each other

in a subdued fashion. Some Unionists got up a flirtation with some Nationalists. There was squeezing of hands in corners and a kiss or two over the policy of Devolution. Mr. Wyndham was Chief Secretary at the time, and ought to have acted as chaperon; but he was remiss, or perhaps was not unwilling to allow the flirtation to proceed. The Ulster Unionists discovered what was going on and put a stop to it in the interest of political propriety. Mr. Wyndham was succeeded by Mr. Long. The Irish people, genuinely interested in the working of the Land Purchase Act, cared very little about Devolution. The general feeling was that illicit flirtation ought not to be encouraged.

It would be pleasant to record that Mr. Griffith's pamphlet sounded a trumpet-call which awakened a slumbering Ireland; that a new, virile party sprang into existence; that a nation, sick to death of scheming and intrigue, declared that henceforth its reliance should be on itself, itself alone. Nothing of the sort happened.

A few young men and young women in
Dublin, already more or less intrigued by
the idea of a Gaelic Revival, read Mr.
Griffith's pamphlet and won for themselves
a scoffing nickname. A company of
musicians known as the Blue Hungarian
Band was at that time delighting the
patrons of London restaurants with waltz
tunes. Mr. Griffith's young intellectuals
in Dublin were known as the " Green
Hungarian Band." Here and there, in
provincial towns and country places, a few
men in whom the spirit of the Fenians
survived were sulking silently in their
tents, profoundly dissatisfied with the
condition of the Irish Nationalist movement. They read Mr. Griffith's pamphlet
and recognised in it a Nationalism like their
own. It was straightforward. It was un-
compromising. If it did not advocate
the forging of pike-heads, it at least recognised that England was the enemy, to
be fought, not conciliated.

Mr. Griffith founded a party and was
fortunate at the outset in acquiring a good

name for it. Sinn Féin, which means
Ourselves, exactly expressed the idea which
inspired the new party. Ireland was henceforth to shun all foreign alliances, to shake
herself free of the entanglements of foreign,
that is to say of British, politics, and
to become great and free by self-
reliance, self-help, self-culture and self-
sacrifice. There could scarcely have
been found a fitter name for a party with
such high ideals.

In everything else, except its name, the
forming of the new party seemed an
unfortunate enterprise. Perhaps it is
never possible to form a political party.
Parties come into existence far down at the
depths of the nation, as water begins to
boil at the bottom of a large pot. Leaders,
like bubbles, emerge from the depths, are
caught by swirlings of popular emotion,
and carried, glistening, to the surface.
No party begins with leaders or with a
policy. Both come into being out of the
vague, inchoate movements of a spirit
somewhere unseen. To form a party

45

with a ready-made leader and a policy neatly summarised on a sheet of paper seems of all forms of political activity the most futile. Pygmalion was able to give vitality to a statue of his own making, and Frankenstein succeeded in a similar attempt, much to his subsequent sorrow. No other man, so far as we know, ever gave life to a thing of his own creation.

Mr. Griffith was not even fortunate in the environment of his new party. Never in her history was Ireland less inclined to self-reliance. The soul of the country was debauched with doles and charities. An English statesman might quite truthfully have boasted that Ireland would eat out of his hand. The only thing which troubled most of us was that the hand, whether we licked it or snarled at it, was never full enough. The idea of self-help was intensely unpleasant, and as for self-sacrifice! Mr. Griffith demanded a good deal of self-sacrifice from his followers, but Ireland had for some years learned to regard self-sacrifice as extremely foolish.

46

A member of Parliament did, indeed, occasionally go to gaol. But he probably rather liked it, and certainly gained by it in the end.

It is scarcely to be wondered at that the Sinn Féin Party did not flourish. The astonishing thing is that it survived at all. Its single attempt to win an election was an expensive failure. Its daily paper—a very sporting venture—collapsed. Ten years after the publication of " The Resurrection of Hungary " Sinn Féin was as impotent in Ireland as pacifism was in England at the same moment.

Then a totally unexpected thing happened. *Deposuit potentes de sede*; *et exaltavit*——the quotation cannot be continued. Sinn Féin, true to its name, was never, even in the gloomiest days, the least humble.

It cannot be said with any accuracy that Sinn Féin won Ireland. Ireland took over Sinn Féin. Indeed Ireland took over very little of Sinn Féin except the name. The original policy, even the idea behind the original policy, almost disappeared. The Magyars, to whose example Mr. Griffith appealed, won their independence by passive resistance, having learned by painful experience the uselessness of physical force. The Sinn Féiners of 1916 associated themselves with an insurrection, and later on preached the gospel of ten-foot pikes. The original Sinn Féiners were fond of adding to their name *Amhain,* which indeed follows the words Sinn Féin in the poem by Douglas Hyde whence the title comes. " Our hope," they said, " is in ourselves, ourselves alone." All confidence in foreigners was declared to be confidence misplaced, and disappointment would certainly follow it. The new Sinn Féin appealed for a hearing to a committee of foreigners assembled in conference in Paris, has hopes of American interference in Irish affairs, turned expectant eyes to Germany, is not without a feeling that revolutionary Russia may do something for Ireland. Wolfe Tone was more moderate. He only sought aid from the French.

Redmond's attempt to win help from the English Liberals, foreigners of course, was an example of austere self-reliance compared to this. Of the original Sinn Féin policy only one thing survives—the removal from Westminster of the representatives of Nationalist Ireland.

Yet in spite of its apparent failure Mr. Griffith's Sinn Féin Party had, before 1914, at least prepared the way for success. While Redmond and his followers, absorbed in political intrigues in London, were struggling to keep Mr. Asquith faithful to the Home Rule idea, things which they did not understand and had no time to study were happening in Ireland. There was an awakening of national consciousness, which was not in any way dependent on politics, which disclaimed vehemently any political conviction. The Gaelic League, with its Irish language, Irish customs, dances and folk-lore, caught the affection of men and women. The industrial revival appealed to the business instincts of townspeople. The Agricul-

tural Co-operative Society inspired country
people with the idea of self-help. Poets
and dramatists gave form to the legends
of the past and expressed the vague
aspirations of their contemporary Ireland.
Towards all these movements, awakenings,
stirrings, the Sinn Féin Party was sympathetic. It was Irish, and counted
nothing Irish strange to it. There was a
drawing towards Sinn Féin of all those
whose minds were most awake, who were
most active in work of any kind for
Ireland. The Sinn Féin Party, even in the
time of its extremest weakness, had many
friends though it had few adherents, and
its friends were the best and most intelligent men in Nationalist Ireland.

Meanwhile a deepening discontent was
arousing the mass of the Irish people from
political apathy. Home Rule, long promised, was postponed and still postponed.
Always, it seemed, there was another
corner in the long road before the hoped
for city could be reached. Taxation became heavier and heavier. Budget after

Budget brought fresh burdens. Perhaps the English people gathered "rare and refreshing fruit" from expensive schemes of social betterment. Ireland gathered little and did not like the taste of what she got—and paid for. Doubts assailed men. Had the old Fenians been right after all ? Was constitutional effort useless and doomed to failure ? An answer came to these questions—an answer given by wholly unexpected voices, but clear and definite. It appeared that Home Rule was, after all the waiting, not to be had. Constitutional action had been defeated and rendered useless by a bald threat of unconstitutional resistance. Ulster, beaten at the polling booths, beaten in Parliament, took up arms, and, arms in hand, won its way, imposed its will on Ireland, on England, and on the Empire. Never was a clearer demonstration of the truth of what the old physical-force Nationalists had always said. *Inter arma silent leges*. In the end the sword prevails. Never was a lesson more quickly learned by any people. Nationalist Ireland stood bewildered for a very little while; then, angry and sore, turned inquiring eyes towards Sinn Féin, which happened just at the moment to be the only Nationalist organisation which was not seriously discredited.

Even the Volunteers, later to become the striking arm of Sinn Féin, had not originally any direct connection with the party. They were started with the idea of establishing in Ireland a force of drilled, if possible armed, men like the Volunteers of 1778. They were Nationalists indeed, but Nationalists of a strange kind. They professed to have no quarrel with Ulster or the covenanting Volunteers of the north. Indeed they occasionally cheered for Sir Edward Carson, holding that any one who meant to defy England and English law was worthy of such encouragement as cheers could give. The early Volunteers were waifs, the street arabs of Irish politics, no man's children. They might, it seems, have become the children of almost any one who chose to adopt them.

At one time the official Nationalist Party very nearly obtained control of them, and might, but for some accident, have stood in the place of parents. There was a period, just at the beginning of the war, when the whole force might have been enlisted in the service of the Allies. The stupidity of the War Office, perhaps the special stupidity of Lord Kitchener, stopped that. There was a moment, not more than a moment, when they might have been officered by the Irish gentry, like their predecessors in 1778. But that moment passed. The Volunteers were lively children with very little respect for the conventional decencies of party strife. Nobody quite knew what to do with them. Nobody cared for the responsibility of fathering them. They drifted into the hospitable arms of Sinn Féin.

Wise men, if there had been any, might have noted its powers of digestion as evidence of the vitality of Sinn Féin. It had the appearance at first of being doctrinaire, a party of intellectuals;

53

therefore likely to be a little squeamish and dainty in its food. Appearance was, as often, deceitful. Sinn Féin had a very Irish capacity for absorbing anything that came in its way. Poets, Gaelic enthusiasts, industrial revivalists, agricultural co-operators, amateur soldiers—it was all one to Sinn Féin. Even anxious Englishmen, who believed themselves to be in touch with Irish Nationalism when they lunched with Mr. Dillon, began to realise that Sinn Féin was a serious force. How great a force it was no one in England knew, very few people in Ireland guessed before Easter, 1916.

While Ulster was covenanting and drilling, while the parliamentarians were orating with their eyes shut, while Sinn Féin was swallowing whole everything vital and nourishing in Nationalist Ireland, a new thing was appearing in the country. For the first time in history the underworld of Irish labour achieved a class-consciousness. Like other countries, Ireland long ago had her guilds and lately her trade unions of skilled workmen, respectable and somewhat selfish organisations. Jim Larkin—the man's electric personality forced the " Jim " from the most unwilling lips—opened a fresh chapter in the history of Irish labour. He was a bold innovator, a reckless revolutionary, and he was, in the eyes of every one except the Lord Lieutenant of the time, entirely disreputable. English labour leaders did not like him and were a little nervous about his doings. Respectable Irish trade unionists were aghast at the doctrines he preached. Employers of labour naturally hated him and beat his strikes again and again thoroughly, as only Irish employers dare beat strikes. Politicians of all kinds regarded him with irritation and dislike. He careered about Ireland very much as a strange dog careers about the racecourse at Epsom on Derby Day. He seemed too small and too wild to effect much ; but it was generally felt that he ought not to be there. Jim Larkin ignored all recognised kinds of

politics. He harangued Orangemen from
the Custom House steps in Belfast on the
12th of July just as effectively as he
harangued the Nationalist dock labourers
in Cork. For him it was not the Pope
who was the enemy, nor England. The
enemy was the capitalist, the master, the
wage-payer. A number of men and women
believed him. He founded the Transport
Workers' Union ; gathering into it the
worst paid, the least organised, the most
helpless classes of Irish labourers. He
set it in the way of becoming what it is to-
day, the most powerful labour organisation
in Ireland, perhaps the most intelligently
conducted in the British Isles. It is
said of William of Orange that he never
won a battle and never lost a campaign.
Jim Larkin must have been singularly
unlike that saturnine monarch in every
respect ; but he also had a knack of losing
battles and winning campaigns. His
strikes never succeeded. His men were
beaten, again and again, almost to their
knees. But labour, despised and dis-

reputable, the labour of the lowest depths, became a force in Irish life.

Volunteering was all the fashion in Ireland when Jim Larkin worked there; and he was not to be outdone by any politician, Unionist or Nationalist. He established and drilled a force of his own and called it the Citizen Army. The war clouds, threatening devastating tempest, were already gathering in Central Europe. Ireland was, apparently, ready and most anxious to fling herself into a battle of any kind. Besides supplying men in large numbers to the Imperial, the Regular, Army, she had on foot no less than four private armies of her own—the Ulster Volunteers, the National Volunteers, the Irish Volunteers, and the Citizen Army. Whatever she became later, Ireland was then no city of refuge for distressed pacifists. In a country wholly given over to volunteering even Tolstoi might have been militarised. Whatever side Ireland joined, it seemed certain that she would take part in any fighting that was going, so intensely military was her spirit.

The Citizen Army very soon faded away. In its brief history there is only one incident which interests us now. It quarrelled with the Irish Volunteers, ostensibly over the use of certain halls for drill, really because there was a deep-reaching division, a definite difference of aim and purpose, between Nationalism like that of Sinn Féin and Larkin's labour organisation. Sinn Féin, doctrinaire and intellectual, with its ideal of national greatness, admired and advocated the economics of List. For Jim Larkin and his labour party Karl Marx was not sufficiently advanced. To the believers in Sinn Féin Ireland was all. Nothing else mattered.

"Shall mine eyes behold thy glory, O my country,
shall mine eyes behold thy glory ? "

To the casual labourer, dwelling in a foul slum, half-starved, with a pitiful uncertain wage, " the dear dark head " was like a savoury, a stuffed olive, very nice at the end of a good dinner, but irritatingly worse than unsatisfying when there was no other dinner at all. The bickering between the two bodies of Volunteers might very easily have been the beginning of an enduring antagonism between Sinn Féin and Labour.

Jim Larkin disappeared, to be hunted, so we are told, from one corner of the world to another, a modern Ishmael, with every man's hand against him. His place as leader of the Irish Labour movement was taken by James Connolly, an abler and, I suppose, a greater man.

Jim Larkin never felt the attraction of Sinn Féin. Connolly did. That fact explains much which happened afterwards and is the key to any true understanding of the condition of Ireland to-day. Sinn Féin was a magnet. It drew towards it all insurgent spirits. It disturbed the compasses by which even the soberest men in Ireland tried to guide their lives. It affected Connolly powerfully and strangely. In his mind the internationalism of Socialist Labour mingled with a narrow

nationalism of Irish patriotism. They are oil
and water, but in Connolly they mixed.
And the man's fierce enthusiasm gathered
strength from both sources. In him the
opposing principles did not neutralise each
other. He suffered from no Hamlet mood
of philosophic impotence, the common fate
of those who feel too many things and see
too much. But while Sinn Féin drew
Connolly into its nationalism, that
nationalism was not unaffected. The Dublin
strike of 1913, a long-drawn struggle in
which the workers suffered much and were
beaten, awakened the minds of many men
to the meaning of the Irish Labour movement. Its spirit became intelligible. Its
idealism was recognisable for the first
time by those outside. Sinn Féiners like
Pearse saw that the Kathleen ní Houlahan
of their hearts' desire did not always walk
clad in stately robes as a Celtic queen or
even in the shawls and crimson petticoats
of a Connaught peasant. She might wear,
did wear, the tattered, draggled garments
of the Dublin slums, and was the more

beautiful because of the filth which hung around her.

There were Sinn Féiners, more keenly intellectual, more logically-minded, than Pearse, who felt the essential difference between national patriotism and class loyalty. There were Irish Socialists who refused to follow Connolly, who saw in his nationalism a betrayal of Labour. But the drawing together of Sinn Féin and Labour was close enough. There was cross fertilisation and fruit. The fruit was the insurrection of Easter week, 1916.

Even now, more than three years afterwards, it is exceedingly difficult to understand that insurrection. Judged by any of the ordinary standards of life the taking up of arms in Dublin was madness. The rising never had the faintest prospect of success. The leaders certainly knew, even the humblest of the rank and file must have expected, that disaster was inevitable. The heads of the Sinn Féin Party understood, for—so it appears—they did their utmost up to the very last moment to prevent the rising. No doubt we shall know some day, but we do not know yet, just what was felt and said by Professor John MacNeill and Mr. Arthur Griffith when they faced the crisis ; but the belief gathers strength that the Sinn Féiners and Volunteers were rushed into their active rebellion by Connolly and Pearse.

What did these men mean ? What hope, if any, lured them on ? What passion impelled them ?

We know that for Connolly the collapse of international socialism at the beginning of the war was a bitter disappointment. Everywhere, in France, in Belgium, in England, in Germany, patriotism, which was supposed to be dead among the workers, arose, shook her locks, and went forth to battle. The sense of class brother-hood disappeared like the morning mist of a summer day. The sense of race kinship and national unity showed itself as strong as ever in the world's history. The whole fabric of a dream castle tottered, crumbled, fell. Connolly saw everywhere workers,

the oppressed, insurgent workers, marching
out obediently to slay each other—not only
marching obediently, but marching gladly.
Of the great world-wide strike, the myriad
voiced " No," which might have rendered
war for ever impossible, there was no sign
whatever. Did he dream that even then,
nearly two years afterwards, he might
kindle in the streets of Dublin a fire which
would leap from city to city of Europe,
consuming capital, destroying war ?

We know that many Irish Nationalists,
though convinced of the broad justice of
the cause of the Allies, resented Redmond's
attempt to commit Ireland to the war when
her will was not known or her approval
asked. They were bitter because Ireland
had no more chance of declaring herself
than if she had been an English county.
They were the more bitter because for a
while Ireland seemed to acquiesce in this
negation of her nationhood. Irishmen
went forth to fight, moved by Belgium's
wrongs, driven by economic pressure, or
swayed by the simple warrior spirit, for-

getting, as it seemed, that Ireland was a nation ; behaving as though they had been Englishmen enlisted in their own country's own quarrel. Did Connolly, Socialist and Nationalist, did Pearse, Nationalist and Socialist, deliberately accept the doctrine of sacrifice ? Did they believe that by dying they might redeem the soul of Ireland—that only through the shedding of blood comes life ?

Or were they just caught on the current of a river on which they had lightheartedly launched, caught and swept irresistibly forward to the point at which, for one dreadful instant, they were poised on the smooth lip of the crashing falls ? We can understand how such a thing might happen. Emotions renew themselves and gather strength. Things felt in hours of excitement become settled convictions. Words spoken lightly and lightly argued over become a creed. The craving for consistency hurries the speaker on. The plain necessity for making good the boast, the dread of losing self-respect and all respect,

sweep men along until they do the thing
they never meant to do. Was that it ?

The motive of the 1916 insurrection remains obscure. The results, though confused, are discernible. Sinn Féin leaped
suddenly into the position of a great
national party, the only party which could
command the respect of Nationalist Ireland. From that point on the progress
of Sinn Féin was simple and its success
assured. The older Nationalists of the
Parliamentary party were impotent. Their
elaborate machinery ceased to work. Their
organisation, spread like a restraining net
over every town and district in Ireland,
no longer restrained any one. It was not
that any single man nor any band of men
slashed at the net with violent knives,
destroying it dramatically and suddenly.
It was rather as if thousands of little
creatures everywhere bit through its cords
and knots ; or as if all the cords had
rotted unnoticed, so that when men moved
the net fell to pieces. The Church made
one or two tentative efforts to hold or cow

Sinn Féin. The results were scarcely so much as noticeable. Mr. De Valera stepped aside to argue ethical questions with a bishop or two. He need scarcely have troubled himself. Ireland had made up its mind about the ethics of Sinn Féin. The Church could suspend a curate, but that was all. Sinn Féin, steadily professing deep respect for spiritual authority, went its own way. The Government proved curiously helpless. It threatened and hesitated to fulfil its threats. It imprisoned men without accusing or trying them and then let them out again still unaccused and still untried. It talked with tremendous emphasis about a German plot, and then, though Ireland might perhaps have disliked the presence of such a monster in the country, produced no evidence whatever that the beast existed, not a nail from its claw, not a tooth, not a hair, did not even point to a footstep in the sand. Sinn Féin scoffed openly, and Ireland laughed, a bitter little laugh. Conscription was threatened,

was postponed, and the threat in the end
abandoned. That threat did all that was
still necessary to establish the power of
Sinn Féin in Ireland. The Church, grasping
at the chance of regaining even the appearance of leadership, ranged itself with Sinn
Féin. The Parliamentary party tried to out-
do Sinn Féin itself in denunciation of conscription—and failed. The country, really
anxious not to see its young men marched
off to France, recognised Sinn Féin as its
saviour and gladly gave the Sinn Féiners
their reward. A party which ten years
before had been unable to win an election
in North Leitrim obliterated its opponents
in almost every Nationalist constituency
in Ireland in 1918.

The present position of Sinn Féin is the
direct result of the union between Nationalism and Labour which Connolly effected.

We are inevitably reminded of the
union between the agrarian agitators and
the politicians which gave Parnell his
power. The parallel is curiously exact.
Then, as now, a party of political idealists

gained the driving force of popular support by adopting a policy of economic and social change. Then, as now, the " New Departure " deepened the cleavage between Nationalist and Unionist Ireland. The Tenants' League lost its hold on North-East Ulster when the demand for fair rents and fixity of tenure got mixed up with the demand for Home Rule. The County Antrim farmer, faced with a choice, preferred his party to his class. Almost the same thing has happened again. Jim Larkin was a power in Belfast. The northern Labour Party was prepared to join hands with Labour in Dublin and Cork. From the Labour-Sinn Féin alliance Belfast stands coldly aloof. The Orange labourer, who has shown himself able and willing to revolt against his party leaders, has not hitherto revolted against his party. Labour in Nationalist Ireland has isolated itself by its union with Sinn Féin. It cannot command the sympathy of Belfast, where Labour is stronger than anywhere else in Ireland. English Labour looks

askance at it because of its politics. We
see again, a further parallel, the apparent
subordination of the social reformers to
the politicians. Parnell's supporters in
Parliament were all elected as Home
Rulers, not as tenants' representatives.
Irish Labour put forward no candidates
of its own in the 1918 election. It was
content in every constituency to elect a
Sinn Féiner.

As in the days of the Land League, so
now there is an outbreak of sporadic
crime. Now as then the political leaders
are held responsible by public opinion for
outrages which perhaps they dare not
denounce, which perhaps seem to them
merely part of the price which a nation
must pay for its freedom. It is always a
temptation to those whose eyes are fixed
on a great political change to excuse,
even while they deplore, crimes which
make the way of the opponents of change
difficult or dangerous.

It would be easy to trace this curious
parallel further and even to pursue it

from the present into the future, basing a prophecy on experience. The alliance between Home Rulers and agrarian reformers in Parnell's time ended in a success for the farmers, who secured their end, and a failure for the politicians, who gained nothing. May we expect a similar result now?

Any such prophecy would be hazardous. In spite of the close resemblance between the position in 1880 and the position to-day, there are certain differences which alter the whole situation. The Land League, the force of social revolution which drove the engine of Parnell's political car, was purely Irish. The revolt was against the conditions of land tenure in Ireland. There was no such agrarian discontent in England or elsewhere. The Irish farmers' agitation was as narrowly national, as purely Irish, as the efforts of the politicians. The Irish labourers to-day are in a different position. They are in revolt against the present organisation of society, not only in Ireland but every-

where in Europe. Their discontent and
rebellion are not simply Irish, and no
change in the Constitution of Ireland
would by itself redress one of their grievances or alter the pressure of economic
law. An Irish republic might be, according
to the doctrine of the earlier Sinn Féiners
who adopted the economic ideas of List
would be, a " capitalist State." Sinn Féin
has looked for allies, outside Ireland, in
the Peace Conference at Paris, whose
members are nominees of capitalist Governments, in the League of Nations, nations
organised on the capitalist method, and
among the prosperous *bourgeoisie* of the
United States. These are not natural
friends, they are scarcely possible allies
for the Labour Party. The members of
the Transport Workers' Union are more
likely to seek sympathy from the parties
of international Labour and to find themselves of one spirit with those who regard
national boundaries and race divisions as
obstacles to the brotherhood of man.
Can two parties so fundamentally different

in outlook walk together long, as those walk together who are agreed ?

The difficulty has been felt and a very interesting attempt has been made to meet it. Irish Labour has been asked to look back to Gaelic civilisation and the Gaelic State. There—and not in the Socialist or Syndicalist State of the economic revolutionaries—is to be found a type of social organisation which may replace capitalism. In seeking an Irish republic the Sinn Féiners are seeking the opportunity of re-establishing the Gaelic State and so winning for the workers the good they crave, not by way of going forward, but by going back to an age, golden perhaps, certainly remote. Ireland is a land of dreams, and no man can say of any Irish dream that it is too unreal to survive in the world of hard facts and loud voices. But the primitive communism of the clan system seems very distant. It must surely be easier to struggle forward a little than slip back as far as that.

In 1880 it was easy to draw a sharp
dividing line between Unionist Ulster
and the Nationalist Ireland of the south
and west. Differences of religious belief
and differences of racial tradition made the
task of politicians on each side simple.
The Catholic, half Celtic Nationalists stood
naturally apart from the Protestant, half
Scottish Unionists in spite of the fact that
the material interests of farmers in both
parts of the country were identical. But
the spirit of the Labour movement has
shown itself a powerful solvent of race
consciousness and creed consciousness. For
a while it may be possible—at present it
certainly is possible—for Labour to be
Nationalist in Dublin and Unionist in
Belfast. But will it be possible for long ?

The withdrawal of the Irish representatives from Westminster is a striking
and picturesque part of the Sinn Féin
policy, the one feature of the " Hungarian " policy which the Sinn Féiners of
to-day have taken over from the original
party. It is possible to see in this deliber-

ate contempt for Parliament an expression
of the feeling which seems to be growing
among advanced members of the Labour
Party that Parliament is becoming impotent and that it may be ignored. But
Sinn Féin is not contemptuous of parliaments. It denies the right of the British
Parliament to legislate for Ireland and its
claim on the loyal obedience of Irishmen
to its laws. An Irish Parliament, freely
elected under a Republican Constitution,
would be a different matter altogether.
Sinn Féin is troubled with no doubts about
the value of representative government.
It is still believed in Nationalist Ireland
that elected men are capable of expressing
in the form of legislation the wishes of the
electors. The ballot boxes are still regarded as the means by which the people
enforce their will, and the assembling of
elected men as the way to democracy.
But this is exactly what thoughtful members of Labour parties everywhere are
beginning to doubt. To them parliaments already seem anachronisms. Re-

presentative government has no more "divine" right than kings were once supposed to have. Parliaments may survive for a while, as the Monarchy survives; but it is felt that the real seat of power is elsewhere, in the committee-rooms of trade unions perhaps, or in workmen's councils. This doubt, half expressed, not yet very widely realised, is as different as possible from Sinn Féin's plain denial of the right of one particular parliament to legislate for one particular country.

Ireland, it seems, is like Rebecca when the Lord heard her prayer and she conceived.

"The children struggled within her . . . and the Lord said unto her: Two nations are within thy womb and two manner of people shall be separated from thy bowels."

Ought we to listen further to the oracle?

"And the one people shall be stronger than the other people. And the elder shall serve the younger."

Is Irish Nationalism Esau, red and hairy, who came out first? Is Irish Labour

Jacob, whose hand took hold upon his brother's heel ? Long afterwards, according to the ancient story, Esau cried with a great and exceeding bitter cry and he said : " Is he not rightly called Jacob (the supplanter), for he hath supplanted me these two times ? "

CHAPTER III

THE ISLAND OF SAINTS—IRELAND'S RELIGION

THE sentimental Catholic—Roman or
Anglican—looks at Ireland with friendly
eyes. It is for him the one country in
Western Europe which has preserved the
faith, in which simple piety is still a great
power in shaping life, in which all sweet
observances are honoured, in which men as
well as women still kneel before altars and
still pray. Till quite lately Russia shared
with Ireland the affections of the Catholic-
minded. But Russia fell suddenly from
grace, and now Ireland alone remains, the
single land which has escaped the blight
of materialism, where the hard sun of
secular thinking has not dried the glistening

dewdrops from the gossamer threads of faith.

They come to Ireland sometimes, these Anglo-Catholic priests and new English converts to the Roman Church. Oftener they content themselves with a distant view of our country and its people. Either way they are satisfied. Their souls, troubled with much thought and many questionings, discover among us that fragrance of simplicity, that garden scent which they have sought in vain to create for themselves by burning in closed rooms the pastilles of sophisticated piety. They delight to find that we hold unaffectedly the faith which they have reached by much effort, to which they cling desperately. In this they are not unlike the neo-Pagans of literary sympathies who see in Ireland the last home of the old fairy lore, a land in which forgotten deities of air and earth and sea are still honoured at holy wells and under thorn trees, still preside over the mysteries of childbirth and control the coming of the butter when women churn.

IRELAND'S RELIGION

It is strange that Ireland should be recognised as a spiritual home both by neo-Catholics and neo-Pagans, people alike only in this, that sentiment is dearer to them than logic. For Ireland—so the plain man supposes—can scarcely be faithful both to the magic of Druidism and the Gospel of Christ; cannot well pay equal honour to Dana and the Virgin Mother. Yet Ireland's lovers, these souls which gather to us from foreign lands, are conscious of no discord. The same admirer will sometimes himself be both Catholic and Pagan. He will watch the wayfarer on an Irish road bare his head and make swift signings of the Cross when the Angelus sounds from a church bell. Tears of thankfulness will be very near his eyes, and—if he happens to know them—he will murmur the lines of Seumas O'Sullivan :

"I cannot pray as Christians used to pray,
    For I have seen Lord Angus in the woods."

Curiously enough—and this is but one example among many of how little logic has to do with life—there is much to be said for both views of Ireland. We have retained more of the paganism of our remote ancestors than most peoples. And we are, whatever Church we belong to, definitely and strongly Christian. The evidence of our paganism must be sought for a little below the surface of our life and will be found, perhaps, only by those who search with sympathy. The evidence of our Christianity is plain and unmistakable.

We are, for instance, a church-going people. Attendance at Mass or matins is not indeed a proof of deep spirituality, but it is evidence that religion has a certain grip upon our lives. A few years ago people in England, with a taste for statistics, used occasionally to work out an amateur census of church-going, counting in some particular locality the number of people who passed through the doors of the churches on a Sunday. Such reckonings were never made in Ireland. The figures would not be worth the trouble required to get them. No one would think of counting the number of people who wear hats out of doors ; though there are a few persons who prefer to go bare-headed.

An Irishman once took a young footman over to London with him. On Sunday morning, being careful about the spiritual interests of his servant, he asked the man if he wished to go to Mass, offering to tell him how to reach the Brompton Oratory. The footman was quite confident that he could find the way himself.

" I'll just step into the street," he said, " and then follow the crowd."

In Ireland the policy of following the crowd on a Sunday morning would certainly bring the stranger safely to a place of worship of some sort ; throughout three-fourths of Ireland to a church in which Mass is duly said. So far it is plain that we are a religious, even a very religious, people.

It is often said, by the envious, that Irish Roman Catholics only go to church because they are threatened with dreadful

penalties if they stay away; and I suppose that there are punishments attached
to the neglect of public worship. In the
same way it is said, by way of reproach,
that Mahomet propagated his religion
by the sword. That is, apparently, true.
But before you can propagate a religion
by a sword you must get a sword, several
swords, and several people who believe
your religion to use the swords. So,
before you can enforce church attendance
by threats of punishment hereafter you
must have persuaded people of the reality
of the punishment and your power to
inflict it. The important thing is that in
Ireland most people believe that it will be
uncomfortable for them hereafter if they
do not go to church now. And that is a
religious belief, a kind of faith; for faith
is the substance of things not seen, and
none of us have seen what goes on in that
other world where the punishments will
be inflicted and the prizes awarded.

But Christianity, as taught by the
Apostles and many others besides the

Apostles, requires something more than
formal acts of worship on Sundays and
holy days of obligation. According to
some teachers, it requires of a man that he
should not eat meat on Fridays. According
to other teachers, a minority, it requires
that he should never drink wine at all, on
Friday or any other day. According to
almost all teachers, it requires that if he
marries a wife he shall keep him only
unto her so long as they both shall live.
Thus Christianity imposes certain rules of
conduct and insists that a man shall live
his life after a certain pattern. Here again
Ireland responds to the test very well.
We do not, any of us, succeed in reproducing perfectly the pattern recognised as
set for us. If we did, Ireland would certainly
deserve the title " Island of Saints," and
would probably be a very unpleasant place
to live in. But—whether more than other
men or not I do not know—we do recognise
supernatural rules of conduct. Religion
is in our lives a formative power, a really
effective force. In some matters we are

astonishingly successful in keeping the rules we recognise as binding. Those of us who think it wrong to eat meat on Fridays very seldom do eat it, without special permission from a bishop. Those who think that Christ damned alcohol—making perhaps a kind of lemonade at Cana in Galilee—are actually strict teetotalers, and will not let even a bishop absolve them from their vows. There is so little adultery in Ireland, and Divorce Court proceedings are so rare, that we are fully entitled to boast of the distinctive purity of our people.

Even when we fail to live up to the rules laid down for us, we still admit that the rules are binding and that our transgressions are perilous. Profane swearing, for instance, is reckoned to be wrong by, I think, all Christian teachers. No one, not even the most enthusiastic lover of Ireland, will maintain that no Irishman ever says the word " Damn " in a casual manner without considering its proper meaning. But the Irishman, differing here

from the Englishman or the Scot, knows
that he is doing wrong when he is betrayed
into a sudden curse. Being religious he
realises that he is running a serious risk.
A small farmer was greatly troubled one
spring by the sheep of a neighbour who
would not keep his fences in proper repair.
The creatures, with their lambs behind
them, pushed their way into a garden and
devastated a plantation of young cabbages.
They trespassed on a meadow of first crop
hay and dragged up the growing grass by
the roots. All day long, for many con-
secutive days, the sufferer found himself
obliged to leave his work and spend
valuable time in chasing the sheep from
his land. He swore from time to time.
Perhaps even Job might have cursed something besides the day of his birth if he had
been so tormented. One evening this
farmer confided his grief and trouble to
a friend.

" God forgive me," he said, " I have my
soul nearly damned, cursing them sheep."

That was the thing which vexed him

most ; worse than the depredations of the sheep, worse than the loss of time, was the fact that in his anger he had imperilled his immortal soul.

That man was perhaps exceptional— what the Scottish Puritans of the eighteenth century would have called " a tender professor." But for almost all Irishmen sin is still simply and unmistakably sin. Right and wrong do not melt off into each other, changing from white to black through indistinguishable shades of grey. They are things apart, between which there is no reconciliation. We see sin as it appeared to men like Bunyan. We do not attach any meaning to the saying that to understand all is to excuse all.

We accept our rules of life from authority. We want to be told plainly what is right and what is wrong. We prefer a categorical " Do " or " Do not " to a vague large statement of guiding principle. Catholic and Protestant are alike in this. We require an infallible guide, whether it be Church or Bible. We detest the trouble of seeking out ways for ourselves and the uncertainty which haunts such search. In civil and political life we are all of us rebels. The very fact that a law is a law is inducement enough to break it, and a policeman, in other societies a protecting friend, is for us a public enemy. In religion our spirit is not at all of this kind. There we like authority. The sterner it is the more we love it, and we ask nothing better than rules for the regulation of the minutest details of our lives.

Our unfailing recognition of the Divine interest in common things witnesses to our sincere belief that the spiritual and material worlds are very near to each other. " With the help of God," a man says, " I'll start in at digging the potatoes to-morrow." Or " It's the mercy of God that the rain held off till I had the hay in cocks." And the man who uses such phrases means them and is not ashamed to let it be seen that he means them.

We attach enormous importance to religious observances. A maid seeking a situation will inquire how far the house of her employer is from the nearest church. She wants to be sure that she can go to Mass regularly, that she will not be kept at home by the fear of a long walk in wet weather. A gardener or groom will accept lower wages for the sake of getting near a church which his children can attend and a school where he can be sure that they will be taught their catechism.

Yet, and this at first sight seems an odd thing, Ireland is very little interested in religion. Conversion from one faith to another is extremely rare; which may be a sign of great faithfulness and loyalty, but is much more likely to be the result of general apathy. If any one does venture to step across the boundary line and pass from one church to another he is, very naturally, regarded as a renegade by the members of the community which he has left. But, what seems unnatural, he is very coldly received by the church he has

joined. No one in Ireland even pretends
to regard converts as sheep once lost now
happily brought safe to fold; prodigals
for whose sake we should make merry
and be glad. On the contrary, the poor
convert, who has perhaps gone through
much spiritual suffering, is looked upon as
a thoroughly untrustworthy person. A
man, so we feel, who would desert his
church—even to join our own—might do
anything, rob a widow or burn down an
orphanage. We decline to see any merit
in spiritual questioning, whatever answer
comes to light.

There have, indeed, always been some
enthusiasts in whom a missionary spirit
existed, who dreamed of an Ireland turned
Protestant, or an Ireland purely Catholic ;
but the common sense of both communities
is against them, and their efforts have been
singularly barren of results. The churches
have stood for centuries in sullen opposition. They have possessed, turn about,
wealth and political power. They have
denounced each other and anathematised

each other's creeds. They have not made converts. Census after census shows the proportion of Catholics and Protestants substantially unchanged. Neither the pressure of the Penal Laws in the eighteenth century nor the efforts of Protestant propagandists in the nineteenth were effectual in bribing or luring the Roman Catholics from their faith. Neither the spiritual isolation which is their lot in many parts of Ireland nor the harassing sense that they are in some ways strangers in their own land has shaken the devotion of the Irish Protestant to his Protestantism. We have attained a religious stability which would be simply impossible in a people deeply interested in religion.

Our dislike of conversion is illustrated by the fact that we have always been unwilling to persecute. Ireland is singular among European nations in possessing no martyr roll. Smithfield fires were never lit among us. Neither Protestant nor Catholic cherishes bitter memories of a St. Bartholomew's day. It would be

own ritual, its own government, its own monasticism. In its cycle of church seasons it was unique. Its hymns and psalm singing, its tonsure, its architecture, were all its own, unlike those of any other church. Its monks were neither Benedictine nor Basilian. Its hermits learnt their lessons neither from Nitria nor Mount Athos. It had its schools and scholars, its saints whose names we still revere, though we have long ceased to understand their lives. It sent its missionaries abroad, apostles of an evangel and a culture strange in the lands to which they went. About its creed and doctrines we can but guess, knowing little except that it was neither Catholic nor Protestant.

That Church, immeasurably rich in spiritual promise, failed and disappeared, leaving no trace behind it save a few ruined buildings to be gaped at by antiquaries and a bundle of manuscripts for the inspection of scholars and artists. Neither Catholic nor Protestant can claim to be the legitimate descendant, the spiritual offspring of that Irish Church. The accidents of history, like incalculably falling stones, blocked the path of its advance. The chance ravenings of pirates checked its development. Men who were not of its spirit sat down in its high places. And now a Church which might have changed the face of Christendom is scarcely even a memory, is no more than a thing of interest for curious minds.

Is it fanciful to see in the failure of that native Church the explanation of Ireland's singular religious position to-day ? Are we faced with a simple case of arrested development ? So a flower, whose early bud has been cropped by some passing sheep, lives on, but tries to flower no more. So a young fir tree, whose leading shoot is broken, grows and spreads, but does not grow to its full height and fails to attain the lofty symmetry for the sake of which it was planted. So we sometimes see a boy give every promise of a brilliant future. His mind is bright and eager. He advances swiftly, till suddenly there comes a stop.

His body remains healthy and his muscles sound ; but an inexplicable dulness settles down upon his spirit. He is last instead of first, and in after years, when others have grown, he, in form a man, remains in mind a child.

I once knew an Englishwoman, much interested in religion, a devout member of her national Church. We fell to talk one day about the Church of Ireland, the modern Church of Ireland, that rigid, somewhat arid branch of the Anglican communion to which I belong. She quoted a verse from the Song of Solomon : " We have a little sister and she hath no breasts. What shall we do for our sister in the day when she shall be spoken for ? " Perhaps if she had known Ireland better than she did, that lady might have widened the application of her words and used them of all our churches, of religion itself in this island of saints, which for more than a thousand years has produced no saint. For it seems as if our religion, sincere and simple as it is, lacks that " superb abundance " of which Browning writes ; as if in its austerity it were too virginal, so that men, though faithful, have not loved it passionately ; as if its babes were all bottle-fed, cannot suck from their mother milk which she has not to give, and so do not grow lusty and strong as other babes, who come in time to beat with chubby fists the face of their mother in rough rebellion, which she delights in though it pains her because it is the evidence of the fulness of life which they have drawn from her.

The few among us who stand outside our churches altogether, who view religion with cool, dispassionate eyes, say that it is well for us that we are as we are. To them, as to Gibbon's philosopher, all creeds are equally false, things of little moment. But in the spirit of Gibbon's statesman they hold that all churches are equally useful, and see in our simple faith and ready obedience a safeguard against revolution and violent change. It is easy to understand their position, even to sympathise with their hope for continued submission and stability. The great world, the Europe east of our shores and the America west of them, is once again, as many times before, in the grip of great ideas, is being spiritually ravished by angels or devils, is God-possessed or demon-ridden. Vast forces, incalculable, splendid, terrible, rend and strive. The noise of the conflict comes to us. The threat of it is at our doors. Between us and many strange perils stands our religion, on guard. Perhaps we shall escape again, as we escaped the formative tyranny of Roman Law, the feudalism of Frankish chivalry, the bursting spring of the Renaissance, the inspired mutiny of the Reformation. Perhaps we shall remain alone, a little sister with no breasts, unspoken for, secure in our timid virginity. It is possible to hope for such a continuation of our island history.

But it is possible also, it is surely permissible also, to hope that from among us will come some new Saint Brendan, who for the sake of adventure, in expectation of discovering at last the blessed islands, will gladly leave security behind and venture forth, divinely mad, across the great ocean in his coracle.

Which, after all, is faith—the obstinate muttering of old creeds in sheltered, sacred places, or the conviction that somewhere beyond the tossing perils there is God ?

For so many centuries we have been patient and submissive, have believed where others questioned, obeyed where others rebelled, preserved our barren virginity when others teemed with life. Is it wrong to hope that at last there may come from us, in time of need, the man who can redeem the world ? He will be a heretic of course ; but not a heretic after the old fashion, challenging speculative dogmas of theology. For the modern world there is no new birth in the statements or the contradictions or in the interpretations of metaphysical truths about the Godhead and humanity of the Saviour or His presence here and there in rite and sacrament.

100

It seems that to-day men need not so much assurance about a world to come as an answer to the pressing riddle of the world which now is, the key word which will enable us to make sense out of the baffling cryptogram of life. Perhaps, because in a way we have been faithful to Him, some Irishman may find that word among those which the Master spoke. Such a one, no doubt, will see suddenly illuminated an old saying, long familiar, long disregarded, and recognise in it the Gospel which we want : " Blessed are ye poor." If he saw that and believed it he would be a heretic indeed. Churches timidly convinced of the need for possessing would cast him out straightway. A world, ravenous for wealth, would laugh at him angrily. But he would know. After a while some, trembling, would begin to doubt. Then doubting and fearing, would believe. Then, in the end, know.

CHAPTER IV

—— AND SCHOLARS—IRELAND'S CULTURE

IRELAND once possessed a culture of her own.

This is an article of faith and we cling to it with affectionate fervour. It is, perhaps, the only belief that is common to all of us. Differing about everything else in heaven or earth we agree in looking back with pride to a great past.

There is something very pathetic in this pride in ancient glory. I had a friend once, a very old man, who was an inmate of a workhouse. His plight was miserable enough and he was lonely. But he retained a certain pride and self-respect. He was not without a comfort which sustained him. He used to talk to me about the old greatness of the family to which he belonged, of which he was one of the last survivors. He told me of the high place his people occupied in the county, of the grand houses they lived in, of how they dined with noblemen, rode out to the hunt on fine horses—the thought of that prancing pleased him most of all, I think—and sat as magistrates judging the affairs of lesser men. In reality, so far as I ever could discover, his family was not so great as he supposed and had never been rich. Its glory had grown in his mind and he loved a vision of the past which was part imaginary. In much the same way Ireland goes back to her past for comfort and pride.

> " Century following century, still at the heels of the nations,
> Poor, divided, derided, the witmark and sport of the dull."

We have little enough now, have had little enough for a long time, of which to be proud. No wonder we claim the right to look far back to a golden age and say " Then, at least, we were great."

But Ireland is better justified in her consoling faith than my old friend was in his. Careful search into the dubious and confusing records of the past does show that we were possessed at least of the beginnings of a great culture. It was our own, as native as our Church. We were teachers then, not learners in foreign schools. In the advance of Europe towards civilisation we were leaders, and the other nations, scarcely nations then, were far behind us. We had a literature, schools of poetry and cycles of heroic legends. We had a legal system which owed nothing to Roman jurisprudence. We had music, and art which in certain directions was already so highly developed that its accomplishments have not since been surpassed. Though originally we were no builders we developed an architecture of our own. We honoured scholarship. We were not afraid of science.

It seemed for a short time as if the hope of Europe lay in Ireland. Everywhere else, from the seventh to the tenth century,

the darkness of the dark ages hung, un-
penetrated by any gleam of light, or
promise of dawn. In Ireland the day was
breaking. Everywhere else there were
ignorance, confusion, indifference to beauty,
no care for learning or for spiritual things.
Ireland alone was awake, her feet on the
way of civilisation along which she marched
with steps which seemed swift and sure.
If there had been in the world then a
philosopher with wide and detached mind,
one who saw and understood, he would
surely have foretold a great destiny for
Ireland. All the signs showed that we
were fit to lead, that our culture, the only
vital culture then, would impose itself
upon Western Christendom.

No such thing happened. In Europe
outside Ireland, our culture had so little
effect that the marks of it can only be
discerned to-day by the peering eyes of
antiquaries. For law Europe went back
to Rome and took nothing from our
Brehon system. Neither European art
nor architecture owes anything to us.

The literatures of England, France, and Italy grew, but not from seeds of our planting. Our tradition of scholarship perished and no modern university traces its descent from our schools. In Ireland itself the promise failed and the advance was stayed. There are among our fields chapels and towers, ruins. There are exquisitely illuminated manuscripts in glass cases in our libraries. There are collections of Irish airs into which musicians of to-day dig for materials, trying not to vulgarise what they take. There are scholarly studies of our old literature and our old laws. There are feverish attempts at revival. But the old culture has not lived and does not live.

The story of this native culture is very like that of the native Church, a story of arrested development. But at a certain point the stories diverge. Religion survived. It was flattened out to a dull monotony, but it survived because we were willing to accept from outside, from Rome and Canterbury and Geneva, alien order, discipline, and theology. But Ireland never accepted any other culture. Her own disappeared. No other took its place.

Our art vanished first, and next our architecture, itself a later development. And the artistic inspiration which failed earliest failed most completely. Now and then in later times Irishmen have been minor artists. The work of our eighteenth century silversmiths was admirable. The Dublin cabinet-makers of the same period were artists. So were the makers of Waterford glass. And these arts were recognisably Irish. They had a national spirit. But we look in vain for the smallest trace of inspiration from ancient Irish art. These men were in no sense the spiritual descendants of the makers of the Cross of Cong or the scribes of the Book of Kells. How could they be ? They worked for an aristocracy which had no knowledge of ancient Ireland, which was indeed genuinely, even passionately, Irish, but too newly Irish to have any tradition of the great past.

107

The same story is to tell of our architects. We built our Georgian houses and some of our Dublin public buildings in a style which was spacious, dignified, and beautiful ; a style to which we gave a national distinction. But there is not the smallest trace in this architecture of any Celtic feeling. That was so utterly lost that when we began to build again in the latter part of the nineteenth century we were wholly unconscious of any native tradition. We wandered helplessly among the misleading byways of pseudo-Puginesque pseudo-Gothic, piling together churches as lamentable as the peasant dwellings built by the Congested Districts Board.

The twentieth century opened with a desire to recover our Irish artistic tradition. Unfortunately the impulse was patriotic rather than artistic. We discovered the Book of Kells and rejoiced, not so much because we felt the beauty of the old work as because we had hit upon a work admittedly good of which we could boast that it was Irish. We began to copy and imitate it without feeling. We illuminated capital letters and twisted lines into mazy knots and believed that we were being Irish. Our ancient illuminating became popular, and since in Ireland we are inordinately fond of presenting each other with congratulatory addresses, we succeeded rapidly in vulgarising the art of our old manuscripts; so that now we cannot even say good-bye to a retiring police sergeant without paying some unfortunate draughtsman to make facile copies of great D's and T's from the Book of Kells.

We awakened to the existence of the Irish stone cross, a thing of grace and dignity. Immediately every village stonemason became busy filling our graveyards with crosses which may be Irish but are certainly neither dignified nor graceful. Essays were written and lectures given about interlacing lines and spirals of old Irish ornament. Straightway the cardboard boxes which contain our scented soap were decked with spirals and displayed aimlessly meandering ribbons of green paint.

No doubt it is right to sacrifice anything, even art, on the altar of patriotism. But we ought to be clear about what we are doing. By imitating what we do not understand we are vulgarising ancient beauties. By reproducing, with the most admirable motives but without feeling, the work of artists we are guilty of the sin of procreating without passion. It is with actual relief that we turn from the crudely imitated Gaelicism which has over-whelmed us to an industry like that of the makers of Belleek cups and saucers who are content to follow the designs which delighted middle-class women in 1860. We may be thankful that it has not hitherto occurred to any one to weave Balbriggan stockings or make bicycles of Celtic design.

The truth—surely obvious enough—is that we cannot again become artists like the ancient Irish by copying the things they did. Since the tradition of their art has failed, there is no way for us to get back their spirit except by patient and reverent study of their work. In some arts, in the making of stained glass and in embroidery—partly because stained glass and fine needlework cannot be popular— we have succeeded in feeling again the old inspiration, and it is possible to discern the beginnings of a national art.

In the failure of our ancient culture art disappeared first. Literature survived longest. External causes, harryings by pirates and invasions of conquerors, affected the poet less than the artist. It does not indeed seem necessary that even conquest should destroy literature, though the intrusion of an alien aristocracy must degrade the bard in a society where the chieftain is the natural patron and pro- tector of the poet. Yet Irish literature and to some extent Irish scholarship survived the Anglo-Norman invasion, and there was actually a poetical revival at the time of the Elizabethan conquests. Irish poets continued to write Jacobite songs and social or political satires far on into the eighteenth century.

There was perhaps in Irish poetry itself, even during its best periods, the canker which would ultimately have destroyed it, even had there been no conquests and no aliens. The art of the poet very early became highly elaborated. It consented to be bound by rules, too strict for life. Its forms were complicated and con-ventionalised. Irish poetry seems to have been doomed to death in any event through mere lack of freedom for development. But what actually destroyed it was the disappearance of the language in which it expressed itself. Irish literature of the old tradition became impossible when no one except a few uneducated peasants spoke the Irish language.

Some day, we may hope, the history of the Irish poets will be written. It will begin with the days when the poets held high office in the courts of kings, when honour and power were theirs beyond the honour and power given to poets among other peoples. The story will go on to tell of poets the heirs of a great tradition, the conservers of an ancient and peculiar art, moving as guests among the houses of chieftains. It will tell of the anxieties and plottings of these chieftains, desperately pressed by the advance of a new civilisation, yet giving attention to the songs of the poets and paying for art in honour readily conceded and gold given from scanty stores. We shall read of poets, later, in the camps of soldiers who were fighting their last fight with little hope of victory; later still of poets wandering from one to another of the impoverished homes of powerless and dispossessed gentry, finding scanty rewards and small encouragement among men whose spirit was broken by defeat, whose hearts responded best to very mournful songs :

> " Sean O'Dwyer na Gleanna,
> We're worsted in the game."

And after that we shall hear of poets by the firesides of the peasants' cottages, men embittered, making not poems but satires, libels, witty or merely scurrilous, on the ways of the new aristocracy which had forgotten the ancient laws of hospitality and the honour due to the men of art. This is the last stage in the melancholy story of the Irish poets who are gone, who have left no descendants, whose art, cherished and polished to conventionalised perfection, has died.

It will not live again, for no inspiration has come from these old poets. The poets of our time are not their descendants. Mangan made a few beautiful adaptations of Irish poets. There has been a small number of good translations. But these have had little influence on our modern poetry. No one has attempted to revive the old complicated prosody. No one has imitated the rhyme system. No one has captured—perhaps no one has attempted to capture—the singularly elusive literary flavour of the old Gaelic verse.

It has been different with another part of the literary heritage of Ireland. The cycles of heroic legend, Homeric in their

114

primitive diffuseness, have captured the imaginations of many modern Irishmen and have been a source of genuine inspiration. Sir Samuel Ferguson, himself a real poet, discovered for us the literary value of our old legends. But Sir Samuel lived a little too soon. Ireland, absorbed and excited by the politics of the third quarter of the nineteenth century, was in no mood to appreciate poetry. The country was too fiercely interested in its own Fenians to have any emotion to spare for the Fianna— the militia of an earlier Ireland. Sir Samuel appealed only to the few who cared to dream about the past. Among them was a man to whom Ireland owes much in many ways, but chiefly this, that he so dealt with our ancient legends as to give them a place in the conscious mind of modern Ireland. This was Standish O'Grady.

Those of us who remember the beginnings of our brief period of literary flowering realise how much the discovery of the old stories did in awakening the poetic

soul among us. The works of Mr. Yeats
are alone proof enough that modern Irish
literature was in the line of direct descent
from ancient Ireland. It seemed for a
moment as if Ireland were to have a distinctive culture of her own again, were
about to develop once more a kind of
literature, perhaps afterwards a kind of
art, peculiarly Irish. The stirring of a
literary spirit in the country came at a
moment of political dullness. The passionate struggles of the Parnell period had
subsided into spasmodic personal bicker-
ings. The passion of Sinn Féin had not yet
possessed us. There was a chance for the
gentler voices of poets and playwrights to
be heard.

But somehow the literary spirit missed
its way. Intensely national and believing
that nationality was the law of its being,
it failed. Modern Ireland, which never
really cared for literature or art, turned
again with relief to worship at the altars
of patriotism and to follow the ritual of
the priests of politics.

" John Eglinton," the most suggestive
of Irish prose writers, has an interesting
theory that modern literature cannot
flourish in small nations. It is, he thinks,
wholly different from the literature of the
classical world in that it is not an affair
of oracles but of temperament. It may
be that he is right in thus explaining the
failure of our literary revival. For our
critics, those who understood or professed
to understand what our poets and dramatists were doing, held firmly to the faith
that great literature is the work of small
nations. They constantly appealed to the
example of Athens with a confidence only
possible to men who did not read Greek.
If they were wrong, then "John Eglinton's "
analysis of the difference between classical
and modern literature may very well
contain the explanation of the decline of
our new poetry and drama.

But a much simpler explanation suggests itself. Ireland, in spite of its spring-
time of promise, has failed to create a
national kind of literature because Ireland

does not want literature of any kind, national or other. Men do not write for Ireland because Ireland does not read. I once heard a discussion conducted by literary men in Dublin in which this question was set : " Why have the books of our literary revival no general circulation outside Dublin ? " The talk meandered on, as talk does on such occasions, among such people. At last some one boldly amended the original question and asked : " Why have no books—those of our literary revival or others—any general circulation outside Dublin or inside it ? " He gave an answer to his own question : " Because every Irishman would rather have a race-horse than a library."

Irishmen dislike ideas, being, indeed, a little afraid of them. Nothing is secure in a country if ideas once get loose in it. Not even churches and parties are really safe. And, unfortunately, it is impossible to have literature without ideas of some kind. They are the food on which literature lives.

Irishmen also dislike erratic person-
alities. We prefer men who are true to
type. We recognise without resentment
the existence of various types and we are
on the whole fairly tolerant. In Ireland
a man may be a Protestant or a Catholic,
a Nationalist or a Unionist, without suffering any serious inconvenience. He may
choose his fold, but he must be a sheep.
We do not like wild animals. And, unfortunately, the man of letters is usually,
the man of genius always, an eccentric
creature who cannot be kept in an en-
closure. He insists on looking at things
from odd angles and seeing them not at all
as other people see them. He keeps on
describing things and drawing pictures of
them, not as we know they are, nice and
clear and flat, but as they appear to him
through distorted glasses of his absurd
temperament, all messed up with each
other. We do not want people of that
kind among us. It is far better for them
to go away somewhere else, to London
or to New York ; which, indeed, is what

such Irishmen generally do. That is one
of the reasons why we do not have and
cannot get an Irish literature.

Also—this is a brutal truth—literature
like everything else must be paid for.
The ancient kings and tribal chieftains
had their bards because they paid for
them with gifts of silver cups and such
things, which the bard, after chanting his
ode, thrust into his bosom, bowing low,
even adding, perhaps, a supplementary
stanza in praise of his patron if the cup
were a large one. Kings and chieftains
paid their fools with nice warm suits of
motley. Else the fools would have gone
out to dig in fields or herd swine, and the
supply of quips would have failed. But
Ireland to-day will not pay either bards or
fools. Homer, according to the ancient
epigram, begged his bread through twelve
fair cities of Greece. Apparently he got
bread enough that way. In Ireland the
literary man would scarcely fare so well
though he posed as a mendicant in Dublin,
Belfast, Limerick, Cork, and eight other

fair cities. This is not because Ireland's spirit is niggardly or because we dislike paying for what we want. We pay—heavily—for our politics and we do not grudge the money. We pay—still more heavily—for our churches and we do not grumble. We pay—most heavily of all—for our horse races and rejoice in the expenditure. We want politics and churches and horse races. We do not want books. Why on earth should we buy them?

But the writers of books—bards or fools —cannot write books unless they are paid. This is a sordid fact. To state it is to degrade literature and to insult art. But the fact remains. In order to write a man must have paper, ink, and at least one pen. In order to go on writing he must have some food, and, for the sake of public decency, a pair of trousers. If no one will buy his books he cannot himself buy paper, pens, ink, potatoes, or trousers. He must either take to some other trade or go away to a place where people do buy books.

When we have finished all our dissertations about great literatures among small peoples and exercised our active minds over race cultures and national arts, we come up against these blank, material facts. Men get the thing they want by paying for it, and if they don't want a thing all the talk in the world will not induce them to pay for it. Denmark wants books, and the Dane will go so far as to pay an English author for the right to translate his works. Holland wants books, and the editor of a Dutch paper will pay to be allowed to publish day by day a translation of an English novel. Ireland—the island of saints and scholars —does not want books and does not get them.

CHAPTER V

I. " The object of the system of National
Education is to afford combined literary
and moral and separate religious instruction to children of all persuasions, as far
as possible in the same school."

That is the statement of the Commissioners of National Education in Ireland. They and their predecessors have
been making it for more than three-quarters
of a century. They are still making it,
so far as I know without a sigh or a blush.
Yet no body of men has ever more completely failed in achieving their object.
The idea of combined literary and moral
education in the same school is actually
further from realisation to-day than it was

in 1831. It can scarcely be supposed that even the least practical of our Commissioners has the smallest hope now of being able to achieve the avowed object of the system.

Yet it was an object worth working for. If the thing could have been done, there might have grown up among Irishmen that sense of common citizenship which is one of the most valuable possessions of any nation, which Ireland painfully lacks. The ideal of the Commissioners was admirable. The actual working out of their system has been a flat negation of the ideal. The children of different religious persuasions are separated in their earliest years and rigorously kept apart. They are not deliberately taught, but by the working of the system they are educated to regard themselves as members of irreconcilable parties whose lot in life it is to distrust and fear each other.

Life itself, that wider experience which follows the school years, modifies the result of the education. It becomes plain by

124

degrees that Irishmen of different religions have some common interests. The influence of the home, even during school years, mitigates the education of the school. Parents have generally a good deal of common sense, and children will play together even if they may not work together. But the result of our system of *separate* literary and moral instruction for children of all persuasions as far as possible in *different* schools has had a disastrous effect upon us.

The Commissioners of National Education are not to be blamed. Their insistence in proclaiming their object, even to-day when such proclamations are pathetic, is evidence of a certain faithfulness to principle. It even seems that for some time they actually tried to achieve their object, though they have given up trying now. They were beaten by the only other people in Ireland who took the smallest interest in primary education, the clergy of the various churches. The clergy were quite clear about it that combined moral and literary instruction is dangerous to faith.

The clergy became managers of most of the schools in the country, quickly elbowing out the layman, who at first undertook this work in many places. As managers their power in the schools is very nearly absolute. They appoint the teachers, though they cannot appoint any one whose qualifications are not recognised by the Commissioners. Until quite lately they had the right of dismissing teachers, at their own will, with or without giving reasons for their action. The teachers' claims for salary must be signed by the manager. Until lately the salary was sent to the manager and by him handed to the teacher. The manager must sign the programme of daily work, which cannot be arranged by the teacher, the inspector, or the Commissioners without the manager's approval. The manager selects the books to be used in the school, every one of which must be submitted to him. In return for these powers the manager submits to the heckling of the Commissioners, who reserve to themselves the right of asking questions about unimportant matters and demanding statistics for which the manager is responsible, though the work of collecting them is done by the teacher.

In this way the clergy in Ireland secured control of primary education and were able to guard the faith of the children. Faith, such is the belief of our clergy, is a plant of tender growth which requires shelter from the faintest breath of fresh air. The clergy may be perfectly right. They are experts in faith and we ought to accept their opinion.

It is just possible that the multiplication table may be taught without religious bias. Nothing else can. Writing, for instance, is taught by means of copy-books, and the headlines of copy-books might easily be used as insidious poisons. In order to learn to read a child must have a book to read from, and once the " It-is-an-ox " stage is passed the reading-book may be the means of conveying most undesirable ideas to the

young mind. Even if the Commissioners of
Education, toiling painfully, had succeeded
in sterilising all the copy-books and all the
reading-books, the clergy would not have
been satisfied. They want, quite properly
from their point of view, the school books
to bear their part in building up the moral
character of the child. They want something positive, a distinct colour and flavour,
in the instruments of education. And
above all they want atmosphere. It is
impossible to imagine a school without
atmosphere, Catholic, Protestant, Secu-
larist, Socialist, or what Mr. Wells calls
" Bladesover " ; and if one atmosphere is,
as the clergy believe, wholesome, any
other is likely to be more or less injurious.

The clergy carried their point against
the Commissioners. The original " object "
disappeared, and Irish primary education
became an affair of strictly denominational
schools. The clergy, as managers, appointed teachers whom they could trust,
chose books which they regarded as safe,
and created the atmosphere they wanted.

The last point gained was the right to teach history. For a long time the Commissioners held out, refusing to allow history of any sort to be taught in Irish schools. Now history is taught; but it is the managers, that is to say the clergy, who decide what the history is to be. The result is a *reductio ad absurdum* of the position of the Commissioners. An inspector, highly qualified and appointed to keep the Commissioners informed of the progress of education, visits a school in the course of the morning. He discovers that the children know all about King William's battle at the Boyne and thoroughly understand that the victory won there was the foundation of the civil and religious liberty of Ireland. He reports that the teaching of history in this school is very good. In the afternoon he visits another school and discovers that the children there know all about the battle of the Boyne, thoroughly understanding that the unfortunate defeat of King James riveted the chains of the oppressor on the

K

limbs of Ireland and commenced an era of savage persecution. He reports that the teaching of history in this school is very good. The Commissioners read the reports with gratification and pay the salaries of both the teachers.

For a long time everybody in Ireland was entirely satisfied with this system. It seemed natural and proper that the Commissioners—who had access to the coffers of the Treasury—should pay the piper, and that the clergy, whom no one wants to quarrel with, should call the tune. While Parliament wrangled session after session over English primary education, passing and throwing out Bills of bewildering variety, Irish primary education remained unnoticed. Children did learn to read, more or less, to the great advantage of local newspaper proprietors. Faith remained unshaken. Commissioners were nominated by the Lord Lieutenant, who acted in accordance with the wishes of the heads of the various churches. Teachers were appointed, and dismissed, by the

clerical managers. There was no education
rate to be paid, and so nobody, except the
clergy, cared what happened in the schools.
Neither the parents of the children nor the
people generally had the smallest control
over education, nor did they wish to have
any control.

The Commissioners, once they understood that their original object was un-
obtainable, set to work to make the best
of existing circumstances. They realised,
far sooner than any one else in Ireland, that
the system of formal examinations and
result fees was incurably bad. They
established instead a system of inspection
which is gradually coming to be a fair test
of the efficiency of schools. They understood, and they were the first people in
Ireland to understand, that teaching in its
narrowest sense, the conveying of informa-
tion to the minds of children, is not
education. They set to work to educate.
It was an extraordinarily difficult business.
The existing teachers, many of them men
of long experience of the old system of

formal grinding, found it very hard to understand what the Commissioners wanted and almost impossible to change their methods. The inspectors were, at first, hardly more adaptable. The Commissioners themselves, in their enthusiasm for new ideas, allowed themselves to be led away by faddists. A whole school might be seen solemnly making little boats out of pink paper or twisting scraps of wire into grotesque shapes. Even Irish parents, usually quite apathetic about what happened in school, became uneasy. The managers were stolidly indifferent, neither blessing nor cursing the new methods. For a time something like chaos prevailed in the schools. The old idea that the teacher's business was to hammer the table of weights and measures into the children's heads was discredited. It was not easy to grasp the fact that children ought to be able to weigh things with actual scales. Time and a certain mental alertness were required to realise that geography is not taught by making a child say over and over again that Constantinople is the capital of Turkey. The new insistence on such things as physical drill and singing, once regarded as fancy subjects, was bewildering.

The Commissioners persevered, learning as they went, and confusion is now settling down into order which gives hope for the future. The difficulties in the way of creating a satisfactory system of primary education are still enormous. Our schools are still starved and ill equipped. Our teachers are still underpaid. The people, deprived of any control over the schools, are still uninterested in the education of their children and still unaware that they ought to be interested. But it may fairly be said that the Commissioners, in spite of much ridicule and almost ceaseless abuse, have very greatly improved our primary schools.

Meanwhile the torpor which kept the whole question of National Education in a condition of placid stability has been broken and disturbed.

The teachers discovered that they were insufficiently paid—which was quite true—and that their status was singularly unsatisfactory—which was disgracefully true. The agitation for better pay could be and was carried out vigorously and openly. The Commissioners were the paymasters and nobody was in the least afraid of attacking them. They had no friends. The teachers formed a union, following the example of men of other trades ; but they were not conspicuously successful in uniting. They, like the children, were the product of our system of educational separation, and it was not easy for men who had come to regard themselves as officers in hostile armies to join for any purpose, even to secure better pay. They did, however, manage to put such pressure on the Commissioners, and through them on the Treasury, that salaries have been somewhat improved. The other question, the status of the teachers, was much more difficult to tackle. It was plainly unsatisfactory that the teacher should be liable to dismissal by the school manager; especially when dismissal meant, in most cases, that no other appointment could be secured. The managers held the power of appointment as well as dismissal, and no sane manager would appoint a teacher who had proved unsatisfactory, for any reason, to another manager. But attacking this iniquity meant battering a corner of the fortress known as the managerial system, in other words an assault on the powers and privileges of the clergy. The Protestant teachers scarcely dared, the Roman Catholic teachers did not dare, to make the assault openly. Nevertheless certain changes were made. The power of dismissal is no longer quite absolute, and the teacher has some security so long as he does his work efficiently.

The Irish public was very little interested in these disputes. Our politicians were even less interested. It was extremely difficult to induce any one to examine the grievances of the teachers, still more difficult to get them remedied. Yet, from

135

the point of view of a statesman, the position was and still is very serious. We have in our National School teachers a body of men and women better educated than most of those around them and therefore possessed of considerable influence. They are in every town and country district, intermarrying with the people among whom they live, closely associated with the life of the locality. They are, apart from the actual instruction they convey, engaged in forming the minds of the rising generation. When men and women in such a position are underpaid, insecure, and goaded into a condition of profound discontent, they are likely to become active agents of revolution, none the less powerful because they cannot act openly. It is impossible to estimate, though it is interesting to guess, how far the present condition of Ireland is due to the influence of the National School teachers. If we had been governed by statesmen instead of politicians during the last twenty-five years, the teachers would long ago have been

treated with generosity and respect.
Justice demanded that men engaged in an
enormously important work should be
properly paid and placed in an honour-
able position. Even if justice counts for
nothing, mere enlightened self-interest
should have led our Governments to remedy
the teachers' grievances before they were
forced to do so by threats of strikes.

The next attempt to alter our system
of primary education came from Belfast.
It is radical, but, so far, purely local.
Belfast has demanded power to levy an
education rate for the support and improvement of its schools, and asks also
some right of control over the schools,
the necessary consequence of a rate. Here
we come on one of those odd paradoxes
which perplex the foreign student of Irish
affairs. Belfast is sternly and unalterably
Unionist in political faith, quite convinced
that Irishmen cannot manage their own
affairs and ought not to be allowed to try.
Yet in this most important and most
difficult of all affairs, the education of

children, Belfast demands Home Rule, self-determination, independence and democratic control. The rest of Ireland is clamouring for independence and self-determination in every other matter, but sternly refuses to manage its own education, preferring to leave that in the hands of a Board and of a single class over which the people have no control whatever. And Nationalist Ireland not only declines to claim educational independence for itself; it is fully determined that Belfast shall not have it either. In the matter of education the Unionist says: " I want Home Rule and mean to have it." The Home Ruler replies: " I won't have Home Rule at any price, and I won't let you have it if I can help it."

The paradox jingles pleasantly and suggests the reflection that all Irishmen are mad. In reality we are not nearly so mad as we seem, even in this matter of education. The northern Unionist politician sees in a demand for an education rate and the consequent popular control of the schools a means of making Home Rule more difficult than it is at present. If he can establish in Belfast, afterwards in County Antrim and County Down, an educational system very like that of England and utterly different from that of the rest of Ireland, he will have placed a fresh obstacle in the way of the establishment of an Irish Government. The Nationalist sees in the suggested reform an attempt to precipitate the struggle, ultimately inevitable, between the Church and the people for the control of education. To begin the fight now is to drag a red herring right across the course of the hounds in full cry after national independence. Ireland would be divided, most inconveniently, along totally new lines and committed to a battle between clericals and anti-clericals. Home Rule, Colonial self-government, and even the idea of an Irish Republic might very easily drop into the background during a contest which would arouse the fiercest passions of everybody concerned.

Meanwhile the educational reformers in
Belfast, much more interested in schools
than parliaments, have what seems to be
a very good case. Their teachers are ill
paid. Their schools are insufficient and
ill equipped. They wish to remedy these
evils and the remedy will cost money.
Instead of petitioning the Treasury for
fresh grants from the national exchequer,
they propose to meet the bill themselves
by a local rate. All they ask is permission
to spend Belfast money on Belfast children.
The thing sounds reasonable. It would be
plainly right, if it were not that the
children have souls as well as minds and
bodies and if it were not established beyond
dispute, in Ireland, that only the clergy
can be trusted to look after souls.

II. The State did not begin to take an
interest in Irish intermediate education
till 1878, nearly half a century after it
established its system of primary schools.
It had, perhaps, learned something during
those forty-seven years, for it started the

Board of Intermediate Education without any flourish of trumpets about "united moral and literary instruction." The new Board was extremely modest. It claimed no kind of control over intermediate schools, insisted on no kind of qualifications of the teachers employed, left every one as free as air in the matter of accommodation for the children, arrangements for holidays, hours of work and equipment. It professed at first to be nothing more than an examining body which prescribed courses of study and paid result fees.

The result fees were generous, which led to one good result. Intermediate education in Ireland became extremely cheap, so cheap that a clever child could be educated at a school without any expense to the parents. Schoolmasters actually competed for children likely to earn good result fees. This cheapness was probably the only good result of the early system of intermediate examinations.

The very idea of education perished in

141

most Irish schools, which became cram-
ming establishments of the worst possible
kind. There was open and shameless competition for places in the lists of successful
candidates which were published and
summarised by the newspapers. There
was actually a kind of " religious " competition, three passes and a scholarship
in mathematics won by the pupils of a
Protestant school in the north being set
over against two honours in Italian and a
first place in French won by a convent
school in the south. The assistant teachers
were underpaid and overworked, while the
owners of the schools grasped greedily
at the result fees. The children were
treated as machines out of which result
fees could be ground by skilful operators.

As if the examination competition were
not bad enough in itself, very limited
courses were set for study during the school
year. It did not pay to spend time over
books or subjects outside the course, so
children were kept going over and over
the same books until weariness gave place

to actual nausea. The unfortunate victims of the system acquired a loathing, which lasted far into later life, for the authors whose work they studied for the intermediate examinations. A clever girl, forced to read the First Book of the " Excursion " every day of her life during the whole of a school year, to study each line minutely, to learn by heart all " likely " passages, that is to say all passages which could possibly be quoted in an examination paper, is educated into a distaste for Wordsworth and probably for all English poetry. This may, from a highly patriotic point of view, be an advantage to an Irish-woman, but it cannot be regarded as a satisfactory result of teaching English literature.

The effects of the system of written examination on the teaching of modern languages were grotesque. I once met a young woman of considerable intellectual ability who had taken honours in French three times in the intermediate examinations. She was an adept in the vagaries of irregular verbs and it was scarcely possible to puzzle her about the gender of a noun. But she pronounced " nous " simply and unaffectedly as if it rhymed with " grouse," and distinguished "parlait" from "parlez" by making the one rhyme with " fate " and the other very nearly rhyme with " Charles." That was the way the language was taught in the school she attended, and from the point of view of the schoolmistress that was the best possible way of teaching French for the purposes of a written examination. A girl will not be likely to misspell " bride " if she has been taught to say it as she says " bride " in English. She may easily blunder, on paper, if she has been taught to sound the French " i " like the English double " e." Besides, it is waste of time and energy to teach pronunciation when the object in view is passing a written examination.

If it were not that the intellectual deadness of our middle classes and the low level of their culture require some explanation, comment on the early system of intermediate examinations would be waste of time. Very great reforms have lately been made. Examination is no longer the sole test, is not even the chief test, of a school's efficiency, and grants in aid can no longer be earned in the old way. The Board of Intermediate Education is now able to inspect as well as examine. It has secured the services of a body of able men as inspectors. The heads of schools are showing themselves willing to adopt suggestions for the improvement of their methods. Something is being done in the face of great difficulties to improve the pay and the prospects of assistant teachers. It seems likely that the members of the Board were all along conscious of the defects of their original plan. The teachers must have hated it from the first. They knew that they could not educate while they were tied to the old courses, and had examinations hanging over their heads—like swords of Damocles in every respect except that they were certain to fall at a fixed date. But reform was a

L

long time coming because there was no general demand for it, and no consciousness among the middle-class parents that the education of their children was being very badly done. Without some pressure of public opinion it is very difficult for a Board to get power to mend its ways; and the teachers, forced to earn money in the only way open to them, were helpless. Our political leaders took no interest in intermediate education. It was scarcely possible for them to do so, for leaders in Ireland, perhaps everywhere else, follow and do not guide public opinion.

The intermediate schools, like the primary schools, are now much better than they were, and Irish parents have a fair chance of securing a good education for their children in their own country. But ignorance of the meaning of education is still general, and the Irish public is still much more interested in politics than schools. We might have better educational systems than we have; but it may fairly be said to the credit of those responsible that we have very much better education, both primary and intermediate, than we deserve or have any right to expect.

III. Ireland might boast, though Ireland very seldom does boast, of one successful educational institution. Dublin University with Trinity as its single constituent college stands high in the world. She has produced fine scholars, has encouraged learning, has educated for more than three hundred years generation after generation of men fit to take great places in the world and able to do great work. She has marked these men as hers, giving them a distinctive culture, forming in them a particular kind of character, moulding their ways of thought. Her degrees have a value, but not merely because they are guarantees of certain intellectual attainment. There are other universities whose degrees guarantee as much and sometimes more in the way of intellectual attainment. The Dublin degree has a value beyond that, because the University confers it on men who have been formed and shaped by the spirit of the University ; and it is recognised that men so formed and shaped are fit for many kinds of work. The Trinity graduate is the peculiar product of his own University. There is a flavour in his culture, a note in his mental life, which distinguishes him from men educated elsewhere.

This is success. A university which has accomplished so much has made itself a place and a name which are not to be denied.

It is perhaps the existence of Trinity College, a visible thing doing work which it is impossible to ignore, which has convinced the Irish people of the value of university education. For Ireland, profoundly indifferent about her schools, has shown herself eager about universities. If our primary and secondary schools had ever in the past educated any one, we should no doubt realise the value of such education and try to get more of it. Because

Trinity College did educate men and we saw them, among us and everywhere else, good fruit of the university education, we grasped the fact that university education is a valuable thing, and then clamoured to get it. If Trinity College had never done anything for Ireland except demonstrate the fact that education is worth something she would deserve well of the nation.

Trinity College is *juxta Dubliniensem* according to her title, but in actual fact stands in the very heart of the modern city. Her buildings, her park, her lawns and gardens, are surrounded with great thoroughfares, through which traffic flows noisily and ceaselessly. Shops, offices, and dwelling-houses press against her walls. The life of the city surges round the College. Yet the College is aloof. The wayfarer who goes through the great gates out of College Green into the quadrangle passes suddenly into a hushed place. The change is curiously impressive and suggestive of many things. Outside, the ears are assailed with a tumult of noises, the shrieking of tramway trolleys on electric wires, the rattle of cart wheels, the trampling of horses, the confused, indistinguishable beating of men's boots on pavements, the muttering sound of many voices. Inside, twenty paces from the street, these sounds are heard faintly as from an immense distance. There is silence, almost. Instead of hurrying men and women, who jostle each other and press forward this way or that, who watch for opportunities to move amid the traffic, there are figures, darkly draped, which pass quietly on broad paths in and out of the shadows of grey buildings among the lawns.

No doubt this contrast always must be between a city and a university, between life and scholarship. Men occupied in business or politics, men stressed with toil, necessarily dwell amid noise and some confusion. The student is apart and his ways are hushed. It is the old contrast between the market-place and the cloister. But for Dublin, the city and the University, there is something more, a deeper contrast still. The University stands and always has stood outside the life of the nation. Understanding much, it has never been given to Trinity College to understand Ireland. The contrast between the silence of the quadrangle and the tumult of the streets is a sign of a deeper separation than that which always exists between learning and life. The University, calm and austere, has not impressed her spirit on the nation. Forming the souls of her own children she has not formed the soul of Ireland. And Ireland's passionate life has not inspired the University. Ireland has won all kinds of men to be her lovers, won them and broken their hearts. She has not, for all her appeals and all her pathetic charm, won the heart of the University.

Yet nothing is more foolish, more contradictory of facts, than to speak of Dublin University as an English institution, an alien thing planted and maintained in Ireland. Trinity College has never been English and is to-day utterly unlike an

English university. A boy educated at an English public school passes from his school to Oxford or Cambridge and is conscious of no great change. He is a little freer, sees a little further; but that is all. He breathes the same air, conforms to the working of the same spirit. But a boy leaving Winchester or Harrow and entering Trinity College, Dublin, begins a new life. He changes his whole outlook. He must learn to adapt himself to a new environment. He ceases to move quietly along the stream of one tradition and finds himself caught in a current, strange to him, which bears him through unfamiliar country. Against it he struggles in vain.

Trinity College is Irish, not English; though she is not Irish as most of Ireland is. Perhaps the herald who devised her coat of arms foresaw what she was to be. He gave her two square towers, battlemented, strong and unadorned. On them are two flags, and the two flags blow different ways.

It cannot be said of Trinity College that

she has been illiberal and selfish, or that
she has been unwilling to receive all Irishmen. Of her own will and even gladly she
has removed one after another all the
obstacles which made it difficult or impossible for Irishmen of a faith different
from hers to enter her gates. For many
years now all her privileges, all her prizes,
all her honours, have been freely open to
any one able to win them. She has made
offer after offer to Roman Catholic Ireland
and has been puzzled by refusal after
refusal. Only she has declined to change
her spirit and to give away her soul even
for the sake of winning Ireland. Once,
in the course of the long controversy over
Irish university education, there was the
suggestion of a plan which would have
altered the very nature of Trinity College.
Immediately, from all over Ireland, from
England and Scotland, from remote parts
of the Empire, there was vehement opposition from her graduates. Their protests
crystallised into a simple cry : " Hands off
Trinity." They were prepared to liberalise,

to concede, to change anything except the essential spirit of the place. And they were strong enough to prevail. Yet the essential spirit, the rational, sceptical freedom of the place, was exactly what Roman Catholic Ireland dreaded.

The controversy over Irish university education is settled now, so far as it can be said that anything in Ireland is ever settled. Three experiments were tried. No one will want to tell again the story of Newman's failure in Dublin, when a fine tool was chosen for rough work and broken in the using. The Queen's Colleges failed. They were, according to the bishops assembled at Thurles, "godless," and that damned them; as godlessness, according to the best theological thought, damns men. The Royal University never was anything but a pretence, an examining body with no chance of becoming a university. Now, after much struggle, we have two new universities in Ireland, rivals of the old Elizabethan foundation in Dublin. They are, as Trinity College is, free to work and develop along their own lines. The youth of Ireland is eagerly pressing into them. There seems no reason why they should not complete the work which Trinity College has been doing, and give education and culture to that part of Ireland which Trinity never reached. They ought to be, and may be, the makers of a new kind of Irishman, clearer-sighted, larger-hearted, deeper-minded than their fathers.

CHAPTER VI

EDUCATION—THE GAELIC LEAGUE AND THE IRISH AGRICULTURAL ORGANISATION SOCIETY

THE most important educational work in Ireland during the last twenty years has been done independently of universities or schools. It has been done by the Gaelic League and the Irish Agricultural Organisation Society.

Governments gave grants of public money for education and established Boards to control and direct the expenditure of the money. Harassed statesmen with the aid of professors devised schemes of education. Commissions and committees of inquiry investigated the conditions of education. Ireland submitted, not very impatiently and not very hopefully ; much

Ireland
Burke
Gen.
R929
8

B   Redmo

R 246.r

BOOK CALL SLIP

Please Print

Your Name_____

_____

Call No._____

Author_____

Title_____

_____

Call No._____

Author_____

Title_____

_____

Call No._____

Author_____

Title_____

_____

in the mood of a little girl whose hair is brushed and tied with ribbons by a careful nurse. She supposes, because she has always been told so, that her hair ought to be brushed and tied. She stands still while the nurse is at work ; but it seems to her a tiresome business, of very little value when finished.

I. The Gaelic League, started by a few young men during the last decade of the nineteenth century, had no grants of public money. No Board of influential persons controls it. It was given no detailed scheme or plan. But it is not too much to say that in the course of twenty-five years it changed the whole mind of Ireland.

Douglas Hyde was the son of a Church of Ireland clergyman, the rector of an unimportant parish in an uninteresting part of Connaught. He graduated with credit, but without special distinction, in Dublin University. At an early age, while still a boy, he fell in love with the Irish language. Father O'Growney was a

Meath man, taught in Maynooth, one of the first of those Irish-minded priests from that college whose influence in Ireland has been profound. John MacNeill came from County Antrim, was taught in a Belfast school, and learned to know and love Irish in the Aran Islands. These three men were the real founders of the Gaelic League. They started the crusade for the revival of Irish as the spoken language of the country.

There were students of Irish before Douglas Hyde, O'Growney and MacNeill were heard of. There was even a Society for the Preservation of the Irish Language before the Gaelic League was founded. But nobody else had ever been mad enough to suppose that Irish, the language of a dwindling handful of illiterate peasants, could possibly become the ordinary tongue of middle-class men and women. No one could have supposed in 1890 that fifteen years later half Ireland would be sitting with knitted brows over O'Growney Part I, O'Growney Part II, and O'Growney

Part III, struggling desperately to grasp the difference between *is* and *tá*, deeply gratified at the discovery that " my cow died on me " is not a provincial vulgarism after all, but a translation of the idiom of a language rich in the possession of prepositional pronouns, by means of which simple thoughts can be expressed in the most attractive manner.

Later on, when the Gaelic League was forced to defend itself against hostile, and entirely reasonable, criticism, its supporters found out that there had been revivals of moribund languages elsewhere in Europe. They philosophised, too, and produced more or less intelligible theories about the connection between the soul of a nation and its speech. But just at first the infant Gaelic League neither reasoned nor philosophised. It was not obliged to defend itself. Nobody attacked it for the simple reason that it was not worth attacking. If it had started with a theory and begun with a philosophy, it would probably have ended exactly where it began, and nobody would have been any the better or any the worse. But the theories came later. The first thing was a love, an attraction to a language, as inexplicable as any other love.

Later on the Gaelic League became vehemently propagandist much as churches and political parties are sometimes propagandist, endeavouring to make things as uncomfortable as possible for stupid and obstinate people who will not accept salvation when it is offered to them. But at first, and for a long time, the League was propagandist as we may suppose the Primitive Church was. Its members were conscious of having discovered a source of light, a way of joy. They were eagerly desirous of sharing their treasure with others. During its years of adolescence the Gaelic League was frequently ridiculous—in the eyes of unsympathetic outsiders. No highly-developed sense of humour was required to see the fun when some young man from Dublin aired in an Achill village a language painfully acquired

from text-books and found that the people,
Irish speakers from their cradles, could not
understand one word he said. The cynic
grinned with appreciation when an Urban
District Council declared that it would have
nothing but an Irish-speaking doctor,
although no single member of it could have
told the doctor in Irish that he had a pain
in his stomach if his life depended on it.
But at first the Gaelic League was not
ridiculous. No enthusiasm is, until it
comes out into the open and bumps against
things as they are. It is perhaps a proof
of the value of an enthusiasm that it
survives the stage of being ridiculous.
Many enthusiasms, strong enough to resist
persecution, wither when laughter blows
gustily across them. The Gaelic League
was laughed at and often deserved the
laughter, but it did not die. Later still,
the Gaelic League was hated. People
who began by regarding its love of Irish
as a harmless kind of silliness discovered
that the language, imperfectly and very
partially learned by most Gaelic Leaguers,

was in some inexplicable way changing the whole spirit of the people. Then accusations rained thick upon the League, chief among them that it was a political organisation, and that it was, in some obscure way, " religious."

Nothing is more curious than the fact that in Ireland " political " and " religious " should be terms of reproach. We are all politicians and we are all religious. We are firmly convinced that political action, of the right sort of course, is the only cure for human ills ; and that religion is essential if we are to escape worse ills hereafter. Yet each association, society, and club which we found must first of all declare itself non-political, and its enemies triumphantly score a point if they can discover a tendency towards politics in it. The only thing which damns a society more decisively than an accusation of politics is the suspicion that it is " religious." It is even more necessary to disclaim all interest in religion than to assert political neutrality.

The Gaelic League asserted, frequently
and vehemently, that it was neither
political nor religious. It did, I think,
successfully rebut the charge of " religion."
It offered proofs which could hardly be
ignored of its indifference to the creed of
its members. Its first President, Dr.
Douglas Hyde, was a Protestant. He
might be President still for all the ob-
jection any one ever made to his religion.
In its determination to clear itself from
any suspicion of religious prejudice, it
occasionally elected Protestants to office
who were very ill qualified for the work
they had to do. It even had little skir-
mishes with priests now and then, dis-
playing the courage of men who have
quite made up their minds that they are
not going to be afraid—a very high kind
of courage, for nothing is more difficult
than to be brave when you are frightened.
Surprisingly little use was made of the
argument that the English language is
steeped in the spirit of Protestantism,
though that would have been quite a

valuable argument to use. Perhaps the
League was conscious that such an argument would commit it to a side in religious
controversy. Perhaps no one felt quite
equal to asserting that Irish, the alternative
to English, is steeped in the spirit of
Catholicism. In meeting the charge of
" politics " the League was not so successful. It always said, and meant, that a
Unionist, even an Orangeman, was free to
join it without forswearing his Unionism.
At one time it used to boast that Dr. R. R.
Kane had given some sort of blessing to
the Irish language, and no man was ever
more fervently Orange than Dr. R. R.
Kane. It received, with the warmest
blessing, members of the party generally
regarded as Unionist. But there never
were many, indeed it is doubtful whether
there ever were any, Unionists in the
Gaelic League ; not because Unionists
were refused recognition and were driven
out, but because they ceased to be
Unionists very soon after they joined.
No one in the League tried to persuade

them to become Home Rulers. Indeed Gaelic Leaguers hardly ever talked politics among themselves. So long as the choice lay between the Nationalism of the Parliamentary party and the Unionism of Ulster or Dublin University the Gaelic League could quite sincerely repeat Mercutio's scornful expression of neutrality : " A plague on both your houses."

If Ireland had remained what Ireland was in 1890, a country in which the Montagues and the Capulets squabbled and bit thumbs at each other over the question of Home Rule, the Gaelic League might have remained what it was at first, what it honestly meant to be, politically neutral. Its Nationalist members might have remained Nationalists, though no doubt they would have lost their extreme eagerness for Home Rule as they became more Gaelic. Its Unionist members might have remained Unionists, though they would have ceased to look on England as the great example of all good things. But Ireland changed. The Gaelic League itself wrought the change. Its influence spread far beyond the widening circles of its membership, and Irishmen of all classes, creeds, and parties learned to look at Ireland in a new way. The belief that it is possible to make us into Englishmen disappeared. For a long time that belief existed and lay at the back of our official systems of education. The Gaelic League killed it. The country awoke to the discovery that it never had been English and never would be. Most Irishmen rejoiced. A few grieved. No one any longer denied the fact.

This is the great work, strictly an educational work, which the Gaelic League accomplished. It has not done what it set out to do. Ireland is no nearer being a bi-lingual country to-day than it was in 1890 ; though a surprisingly large number of people know a little Irish, though the names of the streets in some of our cities are posted up in Irish characters, though columns of Irish print appear in our newspapers. Irish, in spite of all efforts, is the mother tongue of a dwindling number of people. Compulsion in school and university has not revived it among those small and scattered communities who are losing the use of it. It is indeed a fact, which should have given Gaelic Leaguers matter for grave thought, that their propaganda succeeded least or not at all among those who spoke Irish as their native language. They remain for the most part indifferent to the value of their possession, even a little ashamed of it. Those who responded most eagerly to the preaching of the League are young men and women who scarcely so much as knew that there was an Irish language before the League taught them.

I once caught an interesting glimpse of the different ways in which the language revival was regarded by those who learned the language and those who already spoke it. A man and his wife, middle-class people, middle-aged, educated according to the ideas prevalent in their youth, were seized by the enthusiasm of the Gaelic

League. They set themselves to learn the Irish language. It was a task of immense difficulty for them because they had long passed the time of life when the mind is plastic and receptive. They worked hard, submitting themselves evening after evening to a young man who could talk Irish but could not teach that or anything else. They endeavoured to speak Irish to each other and to their children. They even, such was their extreme enthusiasm, looked forward to the day when their whole household business should be conducted in Irish. They had a parlourmaid, a pleasant, intelligent girl, to whom they tried to teach the few phrases they themselves knew. Besides being pleasant and intelligent this girl was docile. She consented to learn that "Dún an doras, má 's é do thoil é," meant "Please shut the door." In the end that parlourmaid left, to be married, I think. Not till then did her master and mistress discover that she had been brought up in an Irish-speaking family, had spoken

Irish before she spoke English, and still found it the easier language to use. The story is not without its comic side, and I suspect that the parlourmaid must have found it very difficult sometimes not to laugh aloud. But it also illustrates the strength and weakness of the Gaelic League's attempt to revive the Irish language. The girl who spoke it from her infancy could not be induced to admit the fact. She preferred English as the more " respectable " language of the two. The man and woman who did not know it— and never for all their efforts succeeded in learning it—were proud of each painfully acquired sentence.

Sometimes those who, like my friends, had never heard the language spoken in their lives actually succeeded in learning to speak and write Irish fluently. Sometimes they never got beyond " Tá mé, tá tu, tá sé or sí." Always they, and others who never even learnt " tá mé," came to regard themselves as Irish in a new and fuller way.

We look back now on the many years of organisation and persuasion during which enthusiastic men and women flung themselves with all their might into the work of reviving the Irish language. It almost seems as if the spirit which presided over the foundation of the Gaelic League were like the father in the fable who bade his sons dig for buried treasure in the field which he bequeathed to them. They toiled, expectant of a pot of gold. They gained, what they did not expect, a splendid harvest. So the League, though it has not made its beloved language the spoken tongue of Ireland, has done a greater thing. It has awakened everywhere the national soul of Ireland.

Speculation over the might-have-beens of history are futile. Yet they have a certain attraction, perhaps even a certain use. The Gaelic League might have done all that it has done without becoming the political organisation which our rulers denounce and proclaim to-day, as they denounce Sinn Féin and the Volunteers.

It is certainly possible to awaken national consciousness without arousing at the same time a desire for a separate national state. The Scottish Highlander, a Gaelic speaker, is national in spirit, a Scot, not a North Briton; but he does not, apparently, crave for a Highland Republic. A Welshman, speaking Welsh in church and home and shop, is Welsh, not English; but he is content to remain a citizen of the Empire. In Ireland the consciousness of Irishness, the discovery of nationality, has resulted in a fierce and extreme kind of political nationalism. Was this inevitable all along?

This is the old question in a new form, the question argued with an enormous expenditure of breath and ink: Was the Gaelic League a political organisation? Were its professions of neutrality simply a disguise, the sheep's clothing which covered the skin and limbs of the detested wolf? The answer is suggested by the fact that the Gaelic League did actually stand apart from politics until all hope vanished of persuading Unionist Ireland

171

to be Gaelic. If the Irish Unionist aristocracy had accepted the ideal of the Gaelic League ten years ago they might to-day occupy a position like that of the Scottish Highland gentry. They might be the leaders of a nationalism comparable to that of the Highlands, a nationalism independent of political party. The opportunity was theirs. They might have grasped it. They did not do so, judging — rightly perhaps, or wrongly — who knows ?—that such nationalism required of them the sacrifice of principle. Their refusal made the end inevitable.

The League's nationalism developed— or reverted ?—into the nationalism of a political party. The revival of the Irish spirit became a smaller thing than it might have been, and—such are the cynical revenges which destiny delights in—the Irish aristocracy did not wholly escape the essential spirit of the nationalism which it dreaded. Who to-day will boast, as men did twenty years ago, of belonging to " the English garrison in Ireland " ? Who will call himself, as a great archbishop did at the end of the last century, a " colonist " ?

II. The other important educational work of our time has been done by the Irish Agricultural Organisation Society. Like the Gaelic League, the Society was started by a small number of enthusiastic men without official suggestion, sanction, or help. Like the Gaelic League, it began with a single, simple idea and developed a philosophy as it went.

Sir Horace Plunkett, the founder of the Society, was interested in Irish farmers, primarily interested in the business methods of the Irish farmers. The agrarian struggle was drawing to its end when he began to preach his gospel of self-help and co-operation. Fixity of tenure and fair rents had been secured. The actual possession of the soil was already passing from the landlords to their tenants. It was a great opportunity. Much was possible for farmers if they were wise. Little real improvement could be looked for unless they were prepared to make the best of the chances which their success against the landlords gave them.

The idea of Sir Horace Plunkett and his friends was the improvement of the Irish farmers' business methods by co-operation. Nothing could be more practical; nothing, apparently, more likely to appeal to men bent, as nearly all men are, on trying to better their position and grow wealthy. There is the sharpest possible contrast between the gospel of the Gaelic League, purely spiritual, almost contemptuous of material gain, and this teaching of better business for the sake of better living. Yet the League and the Society worked side by side in Ireland, animated by a spirit of friendliness. Sir Horace Plunkett was one of the first observers of the work of the Gaelic League who recognised its importance and value. The League everywhere supported and helped to defend the Co-operative Societies.

The history of the two movements is up to a certain point alike. Both began quietly, both made headway only after a period of seemingly hopeless effort. Both made enemies and had to fight for existence. Both learned to philosophise—in other words to understand themselves— only after they had been at work for some time. Just as the Gaelic League looked abroad to what other people had done after it had begun its own work at home, and developed its theory of the relation between nationality and language after it had set people learning Irish, so the Society learned from the methods of the Danish farmers and worked out its theory of the importance of rural life, not beforehand, but while it was actually teaching the farmer to co-operate. Both ceased after a time to depend on purely voluntary support and carried on their work with the help of public money, the Gaelic League with grants for the teaching of Irish in schools, the Society with money obtained from the Development Commissioners. The difference in the history of the two movements is that once fairly started the

Gaelic League leaped suddenly into popular favour and became at one bound an important force in forming Irish public opinion; whereas the Irish Agricultural Organisation Society gathered momentum slowly and has never gripped the popular imagination.

Like the Gaelic League, the Society made enemies; but they were not the same enemies. It was never seriously accused, as the League was, of religious prejudice. Dealing as it did at first very largely with the handling of cream and the making of butter, it was scarcely possible to suspect it of an insidious kind of religious proselytism. Even an expert in controversy cannot distinguish the milk of a Protestant from the milk of a Catholic cow when once they are poured into a separator. Besides, cows, which are bought and sold, change their religion with their owners, holding by the sixteenth century maxim *Cujus regio, ejus religio.* Politics, the cause of many attacks on the Gaelic League, were no more than the excuse

176

for attacks on this Society. It is true that
Irish Parliamentary Nationalists did their
utmost to hinder the work of the Society.
They professed to believe that the organisation of farmers was merely a cloak to
cover an attempt to undermine the discipline of their party. It is curious to think
that members of this party, certainly not
wanting in political intelligence, should
have spent so much time and energy in
attacking a society which was doing them
no harm, while they remained blind to the
forces really at work for their destruction.
They attached, or appeared to attach,
enormous importance to the influence of
the Irish Agricultural Organisation Society.
They regarded the influence of Sinn Féin
as entirely unimportant.

But in truth the accusation of political
propaganda was never more than an excuse
for the attack on the Society. The real
reason lay in the fears and jealousy of the
shopkeepers of the country towns. These
men were prospering, sometimes growing
rich in the most unexpected places by a

kind of business which is of course legitimate, but which is certainly not beneficial
to society. They gave extended credit,
kept running accounts which always went
on running, and worked up to a system of
tied customers. Besides supplying goods
on credit they actually lent money at
rates of interest which not even a chartered
accountant could calculate. The farmer
was in debt, so deeply in debt that he was
no longer free to buy where he chose. He
was forced to buy in the shop of his
creditor. Sometimes he could not even
sell where he chose, for the shopkeeper took
some of the produce of the land in part
satisfaction of debts which were never
wholly paid. Occasionally the shopkeeper held a mortgage on the farmer's
land.

The system was an extremely bad one;
but neither the shopkeepers nor the farmers
saw anything amiss with it. To the
farmers, I suppose, it seemed natural and
inevitable. They growled when they paid,
or promised to pay, high prices for bad

seeds and ineffective manures. But they saw no way of getting free to go elsewhere for their supplies. The shopkeepers actually regarded themselves as public benefactors. They said—and they were not conscious hypocrites—that they supported the farmers in lean years, that without their benevolent credit their customers would often have died of starvation. They took credit for the fact that they never pressed for the complete settlement of an account, that accounts ran on for years, ran on sometimes from one generation to another. I once had the opportunity of discussing the system with one of these shopkeepers. I asked him what rate he charged on long overdue debts, and how he calculated it when small payments were made on account at irregular intervals. His reply revealed a curious kind of finance. " I go over the books now and again," he said, " and put on a pound or ten shillings according as I think the man ought to pay." The man, the unfortunate customer, had no control

whatever over these additions to his
debt.

The men who profited by this system
very naturally objected to a society which
aimed at teaching the farmer better
business methods. They were able to
exercise great influence in the councils of
the Parliamentary party. They used their
influence to injure the Society and hamper
its work. There was a long and bitter
controversy, sometimes in the columns of
the Press, more often out of sight of the
public in those dim places where questions
of policy are really decided. The Society
was hampered and hindered, but it went
on with its work and has won a fair
measure of success.

The days of financial dependence on the
shopkeeper have passed. The farmer is no
longer a tied customer to be exploited.
He is a valuable patron of the shopkeeper
to be served as well as possible. He has
achieved financial independence, and when
he works with borrowed capital gets it
either from a joint stock bank, on terms

which are neither ambiguous nor onerous, or, more conveniently, from one of the agricultural banks which he and his fellows control. He is learning the lesson of co-operation in production.

Here again, as with the Gaelic League, success is not to be measured only by the accomplishment of avowed aims ; though in this respect the Society has no reason to be ashamed of its record. The number of co-operative societies of one kind or another was 947 when the last report was issued. These societies contained more than 113,000 members. Their business involved a turnover of $7\frac{1}{2}$ million pounds during the year. The parent society received affiliation fees amounting to more than £1,700. This is a great accomplishment ; but a still greater accomplishment cannot be reckoned in figures or reduced to statistics. The Irish farmer, whether he is a member of a co-operative society or not, is a far better business man than he was twenty-five years ago. He owes much to the Department of Agriculture, which has shown him good ways of farming. He owes even more to the Irish Agricultural Organisation Society, whose persistent teaching of good business methods has shown the farmer how to win and keep his markets, how to use to the fullest advantage his position as a producer of food.

The educational work of the Society has not stopped short at the improving of the business side of farming. The founders of the Society came to understand, very early in their work, that man does not live by bread alone, that something more is required for happiness than a bank balance. Rural life, not only in Ireland, but everywhere, has suffered grievously from dullness. The young, the vigorous, and the active are tolerant of anything rather than monotony. The best men will face toil and perhaps privation cheerfully enough. They will not willingly resign themselves to years of unrelieved stupidity, not even for the sake of full bellies and warm backs.

The city, with its promise of companion-
ship, with its lights and sounds and varied
interests, lures men from the country-
side. In Ireland the case is worse
than elsewhere because the cities which
called were not near at hand, but across
the Atlantic.

All this became plain to the leaders of
the Irish Agricultural Organisation Society,
and they attempted the very difficult task
of making country life interesting and
attractive. They conceived the idea of the
rural co-operative community, a little
society with a village hall as the centre of
its life, knit together by common interests,
animated by a spirit of brotherhood, not
only careful of its material prosperity,
but taking thought also for its pleasure
and its intellectual needs. Clearly no such
organisation of life could be imposed on an
unwilling people, or a people unready, by
outsiders, however well fitted they might
be to play the part of benevolent providence. Such a civilisation must be the

work of the community itself, growing from a sense of need, arriving by way of many experiments at the satisfaction of the need. The leaders of the Society could do no more than stimulate the desire for a better life where such desire existed, and suggest ways and plans.

Meanwhile, in the minds of men who are thinking much about Irish life the vision of great things grew and strengthened, far outstripping the slow accomplishment. Beyond the village community, itself nowhere yet half realised, there rose " the cloud-capped towers and gorgeous palaces" of a co-operative state, a new kind of social order, sweeter, tenderer, in every way more beautiful than the old.

So, in Ireland, we move from the material to the spiritual, and back from the spiritual to the material again. Of these two great movements of education, that of the Gaelic League and that of the Irish Agricultural Organisation Society, the one began with a dream and by way of its

dream came to business, the practical
business of establishing a politically independent Irish Republic. The other
began with business, the business of selling
butter profitably, and arrived at a dream
in the end.

CHAPTER VII

THE IRISH ARISTOCRACY

THE Sinn Féiner of to-day never quotes and rarely refers to Mr. Arthur Griffith's "Resurrection of Hungary," though that pamphlet was the earliest manifesto of the party. Perhaps he does not read it any more. Perhaps he has read it carefully enough to discover that there is no resemblance whatever between the Irish Irelander and the Magyar. The Magyars are—perhaps we should say were—members of a dominant aristocracy, a governing race which was not native to Hungary. They are—or were—fighters and men of affairs. They had the virtues and vices of a class accustomed to rule. During their struggle for independence they made it clear that they did not mean to be bullied by the

Austrians. Ever since they got the power they wanted they have been making it clear that they meant to hold in subjection the unfortunate Slav. If Mr. Griffith's pamphlet suggests any lesson for Ireland, it is certainly not one of encouragement for our insurgent Gaels. If we must find resemblances between ourselves and the Hungarians—which seems to me unnecessary—the Magyars seem to correspond most nearly to our Anglo-Irish aristocracy, which once asserted itself successfully against England, as the Magyars did against Austria; and then, unlike the Magyars, gave up again the political independence it had gained.

It is the fashion among Nationalists to regard the Anglo-Irish gentry as England's garrison in Ireland. The gentry have sometimes, though not often and not for long, thought and spoken of themselves in this way; which is perhaps not very odd, since one of the characteristics of this class is that it has forgotten its own history. Nationalists, on the other hand, remember history very well, perhaps too well, and must know that the Irish gentry never were an English garrison. England always disliked them and never trusted them.

This class was the flower of the Anglo-Irish race, a race of mixed blood, but quite as distinct from the English as it is from the Gaelic Irish. It was formed by a series of waves of immigrants, Normans, Elizabethan Englishmen, Scots of the time of James I, Cromwellian soldiers, William-ite soldiers, French Huguenots. But the race, and the aristocracy which best exhibits its peculiar spirit, is neither Norman, English, Scottish, Dutch, nor French. It became something different from all these. It became Irish.

Scarcely a book is ever written about Ireland in which the phrase is not quoted about the strangers, the settlers, who became *Hibernis ipsis Hiberniores*. Much is usually said about Ireland's wonderful power of absorbing those who come to her as aliens, of spiritually conquering her conquerors. I suppose there is some truth in it all, or it would not be said so often and so confidently. But if by Irish we mean Gaelic, then Ireland never did absorb this aristocracy or conquer its soul. When the Anglo-Irish race emerges, its character formed, at the beginning of the eighteenth century, it is no more Gaelic than it is English. So far from being absorbed, this race displayed the power of absorbing the remains of that older Gaelic aristocracy which it displaced. The O'Briens, the Kavanaghs, and the others whose names appear in the pages of Burke's books of Nobility and Gentry were of Gaelic origin. But they are Anglo-Irishmen to-day in character, in mind, and by tradition. They did not assert a spiritual supremacy by absorbing the newcomers. They were absorbed, re-formed by a spirit stronger than their own.

The history of the eighteenth century shows us this race governing Ireland, not in the least as a garrison in the interests of England, but, after the fashion of aristocracies in those days, in its own

interests. So far from regarding itself
as an English garrison, this aristocracy conceived the highly patriotic idea of an Irish
nation, holding that it was itself the Irish
nation ; therein bettering the arrogance
of Louis XIV, who only went so far as to
say that he was the State. Its efforts to
govern Ireland were continually hampered
by the enactments of the English Parliament and the intrigues of English officials.
The "Irish nation," our aristocracy,
resented and resisted English interference,
not at all in the spirit of a faithful garrison.
England was under no delusions about these
men. Every one of those eighteenth century measures of commercial restriction
which we still resent was directed against
the Anglo-Irish, and especially against
the aristocracy. All the acts of political
oppression, all the schemes and intrigues,
were meant to curb the power, not of the
Gaelic Irish who had no power, but of the
Irish gentry. Towards the end of the
century the aristocracy successfully asserted itself, became independent of Eng-

land, and faced the task of governing Ireland.

It was a difficult time for aristocracies and governing classes because Europe was full of the ferment of French revolutionary ideas. But the Irish aristocracy did not do badly. It might have actually done well if it had not suffered, for the first and only time in its history, from self-distrust. It was not quite sure of its own ability to deal with the United Irishmen. It allowed itself to be frightened, persuaded, cajoled and bribed into sacrificing its independence by passing the Act of Union. England wanted the Union, not because she loved the Anglo-Irish lords and gentlemen, but because she disliked and rather dreaded them. With the prospect of a long and desperate war before them, English states-men saw the necessity for tightening their grip on Ireland.

Since then England has steadily sacri-ficed the Irish aristocracy whenever it was in her interest to do so. It made no matter what the England of the moment

might be. The England of the Whig and
Tory landowners, the England of the
Liberals of commerce, the England of the
later democracy were all alike in their
treatment of Anglo-Irishmen. Attempts
have been made of late to win the affections of Irish Irelanders, generally by giving
them doles and grants of money. The
money came, directly or indirectly, out
of the pockets of the Anglo-Irish. To-day
England professes to be ready to give
anything to Ireland—except of course what
Ireland asks—but she cynically refuses to
pay the money she owes to those dis-
inherited members of the Irish aristocracy
who parted with their property at her
request.

If this class is an English garrison in
Ireland, it has behaved as no other garrison
ever did and has been very ill-supported
by those for whom it held its fort.

Yet there is some excuse for Ireland when
she makes this reproach. The Irish aristocracy has never been sympathetic with
the " mere " Irish. It has now and again—

indeed often—supplied leaders of Irish
Nationalism. But as a class it has stood
aloof from every popular movement, coolly,
even cynically, indifferent to every enthusiasm. During the nineteenth century
it fought a long-drawn-out battle for its
powers, its privileges, and its property.
It was gradually but disastrously beaten,
driven from post to post till no refuge was
left to it anywhere. But it never made
terms with Irish Ireland, never sacrificed
its principles by compromise.

Such a history left its marks upon a
class which succeeded in preserving its
class consciousness. The Irish gentry are
not to-day what their great-grandfathers
were at the end of the eighteenth century.
They have lost that capacity for
enthusiasm and abandon which made
Grattan's Parliament a great school of
oratory. They have become distrustful
of ideas; for political ideas have been
rampant in Ireland for a century, and
little good seems to have come
of them. A long apprenticeship in

the Imperial service has widened their
outlook. It would be impossible for them
to-day to think of themselves as " the
Irish Nation." They have fought the
Empire's battles in every corner of the
world and ruled for the Empire every land
except their own. They have become,
more than any other men perhaps, cos-
mopolitan in spirit, as their ancestors never
were. The Gaelic aristocracy which pre-
ceded them was driven into exile, and
crossed the seas, a long flight of " Wild
Geese." This aristocracy is no less exiled,
though they linger in their houses and
demesnes in Ireland. They are spiritual
exiles who have gone forth or have been
driven forth from the life of the community.
They are men without a country, servants
of an Empire to which they are able to give
a loyalty unconfused by the mixture of any
narrower patriotism.

Yet many of the old characteristics of
the race remain. We see in them to-day
that same cool sanity which gave their
terrible force to the writings of Swift,

which turned him into a madman at last,
if men can be made mad by excess of
sanity. They remain, what they always
were, devoted to sport, understanding all
life as a kind of sport, more dangerous
than the pursuit of foxes or the competitive
"poundings" of the Connaught gentry
fifty years ago, and therefore more de-
lightful; more thrilling than horse-racing
because the stakes are greater; but to be
lived in the spirit of sportsmen, according
to the rules which govern sport. They
have courage, not only that physical
courage which has set them in the front of
every battle of the Empire, but the courage,
far rarer in Ireland, of the men who will
stand apart from the crowd and smile at
either the shouting or the hooting. They
have that capacity for affairs and rulership
which enabled their ancestors to govern
Ireland for those few years at the end of
the eighteenth century when Ireland
flowered. They have proved their capacity
and their instinct for leadership in the
service of the Empire everywhere, as their

ancestors used the same powers in Ireland. But in one quality, most necessary in the management of a nation's affairs, our Irish aristocracy is lacking. The bitter history of the last century has left them almost without hope. They have no belief in the future of a self-governing Ireland. They have no confidence in the Union, to which nevertheless they cling as to the lesser of two evils. If it were possible to convince them that the future, either way, holds any chance of good, they might do much for Ireland and might save themselves. But they have too much experience to trust the prophecies of enthusiasts and are too sane to see visions themselves.

Standish O'Grady, who used to write singularly illuminating articles about Ireland, lamented the fall of this aristocracy and deplored the manner of the fall because no brave words were spoken and no great deeds were done. From the point of view of the amateur of the picturesque in history it must seem that there has been a lack of

heroic incident, and, I suppose, no poet
will ever sing of these gentlemen as poets
did of the Jacobite " Wild Geese." But
they have not been without dignity in the
way they have met misfortune. They
became involved in a fight which was none
of theirs, the nineteenth century struggle
between England and Ireland. Their
wounds, dealt by both combatants, were
not " as deep as a well or as wide as a
church door," but sufficient. They have
taken them with a half-smile on their lips,
as if slightly amused at the perverse
stupidity of the combatants, as if slightly
contemptuous of both. The almost complete detachment, the absence of prejudice
which enabled him to view even his own
ruin without passionate resentment, gives
the Irish gentleman his singular position
in European society to-day. He is the
only spiritual descendant of the cool, purely
sceptical gentlemen of the eighteenth
century.

Perhaps even now this aristocracy might
lead Ireland, discover a new kind of

nationality, invent, as they invented before and created, an Irish nation; perhaps—if only—and if—and if—— But what is the use of saying " if " ? If tides would cease to flow at our bidding or if storms would cease to rage !

CHAPTER VIII

THE FARMERS

THERE is a story which used to be told
very often about an Irish farmer. He was
a Limerick farmer sometimes, a Ros-
common farmer sometimes. Sometimes
he belonged to Galway. Asked what he
did in his lonely home during the long
winter evenings he replied :

"Sometimes I sits and thinks. Sometimes I simply sits."

It is a well-invented story, and does
credit to the wit of the author, who was
almost certainly a city dweller.

It expresses very neatly the contempt
which town-people have for the intelligence
of countrymen. This contempt is not a
peculiar product of our time. It is as old,
at least, as the Greek classical civilisation.

It turns up in the literature of every country and of every age since then. Perhaps it is a well-deserved contempt, founded upon observation of some real dullness, some intellectual sluggishness in country-people. If so the Irish farmer must be an exceptional person. Judged by the rough and ready but very trustworthy standard of his achievements, the Irish farmer must be a great deal more intelligent than most other people and much readier to grip opportunity by that front part of its head which is not bald. If it is true of him that he spends his winter evenings simply sitting, it must be admitted that he has got more by it than townspeople have by fussing about and thinking hard.

In the middle of the nineteenth century the position of the Irish farmer was in some parts of the country miserable in the extreme, in all parts of the country singularly unsatisfactory. His standard of comfort was very low. He had no security of tenure. He suffered from every kind of uncertainty. He might at any time be turned out of his holding. His rent might be increased. Legislation aimed at keeping the price of his produce as low as possible in the interests of the urban population. The house in which he lived was uncomfortable and inconvenient. He and the class to which he belonged were only slowly emerging from the consequences of a desolating famine. Experimenters in rural economics were completing the work of the famine by turning great tracts of inhabited country into cattle ranches. The prospects were so hopeless that the young and adventurous refused to face them. They fled to America in thousands.

In little more than half a century the position of the farmer has completely changed and rural Ireland has been transformed. The farmer in 1850 was an agricultural proletarian. To-day he is a capitalist. In 1850 he was politically powerless. To-day he shares with the urban publican the control of the local government of the country. His standard of living has improved and is steadily improving. He has achieved a security unknown to the worker for wages. His progress, slow at first, has gathered speed and momentum. The last twenty years have seen greater changes for the better in rural Ireland than the forty years which went before them.

The sixty years of the farmer's progress have been a period of unceasing political agitation and struggle. During that time Ireland has never been peaceful, has never achieved the kind of settled security which would tempt the cautious capitalist to invest his money there. The rest of the country has got very little by its exertions. Home Rule, for which men have struggled so persistently, has remained a phantom, eluding eagerly grasping hands. The poverty of the slums of Dublin and of the still worse slums of some of our country towns has been very little mitigated or relieved. Industries, through the greater part of Ireland, have steadily decayed, and mills once busy have been shut down.

Not even the politicians have gained anything substantial for themselves. The pay they received for their services was scanty. Their other rewards were little but disappointments and broken hearts. The farmers alone succeeded in drawing good, large, wholesome fish out of the troubled waters.

The town dweller must revise his judgment. Whatever farmers may be elsewhere, the Irish farmer is not stupid. He has displayed political intelligence and business ability of a high order. In a community and during a period when agricultural interests were considered entirely unimportant he has secured benefits which place him in a position of security, beyond the buffetings of any chance, except of course bad weather. He has talked very little, being quite content to leave speechmaking to others. He has not expressed himself in writing at all. He has never been particularly generous in his subscriptions to the parties which fought his battles for him. He has not been distinguished by loyalty to his leaders, whom he was always ready to desert. But he has steadily, and very intelligently, pursued his own advantage. The results are visible in the improvement of Irish rural life, improvement so great that Irishmen returning to their native land after an absence of twenty to thirty years stand amazed. The conditions they see to-day are almost incredibly different from those with which they were familiar before they went into their voluntary exile.

Michael Davitt and Devoy, the founders of the Land League, were revolutionaries of a kind familiar in Irish history. After the failure of the Fenian movement they realised that driving force for the political revolution they desired could only be secured by linking their cause with that of economic change and putting themselves at the head of an agrarian agitation. Parnell, after some hesitation, adopted their policy, though it cost him the support of some of the most influential followers of his predecessor, Isaac Butt. In the histories and

biographies which deal with the period of
the Land League and Parnell's Home Rule
struggle the politicians and revolutionaries
are given credit for the great sagacity
of their "New Departure," the policy
which secured for their movement a mass
of enthusiastic supporters. The credit is
deserved and justly bestowed. But no one
seems to recognise that the Irish farmers
showed equal sagacity in hitching their
horses to the Home Rule waggon and
allowing the politicians to drive. Yet
what Devoy, Davitt, and Parnell did
deliberately, arriving at their policy by a
process of reasoning, is exactly like what
the farmers did, apparently without cal-
culation, acting in obedience to a kind of
class instinct.

The result of this alliance was curious
and interesting. The revolutionaries of
the Fenian type wanted an independent
Ireland and accepted the help of the
farmers. The farmers wanted an agrarian
revolution and accepted the leadership of
the politicians. The farmers got what

they wanted. The politicians did not. The two objects were at the time so inextricably mixed that no distinction was made between them. The cause of Home Rule was, apparently, the cause of the Land League, and the cause of the Land League was the cause of Home Rule. A Land Leaguer was a Home Ruler, and a Home Ruler, almost inevitably, was a Land Leaguer. Yet, as we see now, there was a real distinction, and the farmers were all along more or less conscious of it.

I remember a singularly illuminating conversation which I had with a supporter of the farmers' cause. It was during the latter stages of the land struggle, after the passing of the Land Acts of the 'eighties. My friend was one of those leaders of local opinion who never appear in Parliament, whose names are totally unknown to the English public. His energy, enthusiasm, and ability formed opinion in his own neighbourhood. He was content to leave more prominent men to express it in speeches at Westminster and elsewhere, always on the understanding that it was the opinion he created, not their own, which they expressed. Men like this were to be found then, and are still to be found, in every village in Ireland; priests sometimes, schoolmasters occasionally, editors of local papers sometimes, occasionally shopkeepers. They control the local branches of the leagues, " orders," and societies popular at the moment. They count for more in Irish politics than the nominal leaders of parties.

My friend was anxious, if possible, to enlist my sympathies for a new league which had lately been established and was rapidly gaining strength in his neighbourhood. If I refused to sympathise he was still very kindly anxious to allay my fears and misgivings. He knew, of course, that I was a Protestant and assumed, quite naturally, that I was a Unionist, nervous about what might happen to me and men like me under a Home Rule Parliament. He knew too that I was not a landlord and assumed, very naturally, that the issue of the agrarian struggle was a matter of indifference to me.

" Why are you and your people out against us ? " he said. " What does it matter to you who owns the land ? "

" It matters to us," I replied, " who governs the country. Do you think we want to be ruled by a glorified Dublin Corporation ? "

That is a stock Unionist argument, and quite a good one. I used it because I wanted to see what line my friend would take in reply. I confess he startled me.

" Oh, Home Rule ! " he said. " Damn Home Rule. What we're out for is the land. The land matters. All the rest is tall talk."

My friend was quite properly regarded as a leading Nationalist, but he was plainly not a Nationalist in the sense in which Parnell, Davitt, and John Redmond were Nationalists ; in the sense in which Mr. De Valera and the Sinn Féiners are Nationalists now. He was an agrarian reformer and may, for all I know, be a social reformer to-day with a wider programme. But he was singularly clear-headed. Very few men saw the real point at issue in the struggle as distinctly as he did, or realised the high political intelligence—perhaps we should say the astonishing political instinct—of the Irish farmers who consented to shout for Home Rule in order that the Home Rulers might get the land for them.

The rest of the community displayed far less intelligence than the farmers during the agrarian struggle. "The Land for the People" was an excellent rallying cry. The artisan, the farm labourer, the shop-keeper, and many members of the profes-sional classes were quite aware that they were landless, and "the Land for the People," so far as it meant anything definite at all, seemed to mean that they would become in some sense possessors of land ; that if actual acres were not fenced off and handed over to them, they would at all events as members of the community be the real owners of the soil of the country in which they lived. The farmers meant nothing of the sort. The idea of land nationalisation—a dream of Michael Davitt's—was utterly abhorrent to them. Private property in land was to them a sacred principle which it would have been impious to dispute. The debatable matter, the thing to be fought over, was the much simpler question, Who are to be the private proprietors ? To the farmers " the Land for the People " meant the land for certain persons who happened, just at that moment, to be occupying and cultivating it.

The farmer, because he has more political intelligence than anybody else, got what he wanted. The passing of the Land Acts which gave him security of tenure gave him something which he could sell, his interest in his farm. He became a capitalist by the operation of an Act of Parliament. The landlord ceased to own his estate in the old complete sense. He was part owner only, and after a few years not even part owner. Neither the State nor the community nor "the People" received what the landlord was obliged to part with. The farmer was the beneficiary. The net result of a great national agitation carried on for years with vigour, enthusiasm, and self-sacrifice was to take a great deal of money out of the pockets of some individuals and put it into the pockets of other individuals. The landlords saw that they were being injured. The farmers saw that they were gaining. For the rest of the community the whole business was wrapped in a golden mist of fine phrases through which the sun of Home Rule seemed to be rising, red and huge, with promise of a glorious day. But that sun has not yet actually risen to noontide height. The politicians who hailed the day as " not far distant " have fallen from their high estate and ceased to be national leaders. The rest of the community is beginning to realise that the struggle of the last half of the nineteenth century has brought little of what was promised to any one except the farmers. They alone secured tangible good out of the welter of contending interests and disinterested dreams.

We catch another glimpse of the instinctive political sagacity of the Irish farmers when we observe their dealings with the Congested Districts Board. The Board had a limited sphere of work. It was concerned only with those parts of the west and middle west of Ireland where the agricultural population was too dense, where the holdings of land were so small and so inconveniently arranged that their occupiers could not live in decency and comfort. The people for whom this Board worked were the poorest, the least progressive, presumably the least educated and intelligent of Irish farmers. The Board had no mission among the graziers of Meath or the solid farmers of Kildare and Wexford, men who might be supposed to know their own interests and be capable of attending to them. But although the Board was strictly limited as to the locality of its operations it had almost complete freedom as to the form which its work took.

It held a commission for roving philanthropy. It might do very nearly anything.
It actually did try very nearly everything
which could possibly benefit the people
of the congested districts.

The people, the smallest of small farmers,
living under the shadow of a perpetual
menace of famine, watched the early
experiments of the Board with a slightly
amused, not wholly unfriendly, interest.
The introduction of prize bulls and boars,
of the latest and most fashionable breeds
of poultry, did no actual harm to a locality.
The starting of crochet classes, the sub-
sidising of small woollen mills, and such like
attempts at the establishment of local
industries were, from the point of view of
these small farmers, amiable futilities.
They did not really care whether their
daughters made crochet collars or not,
nor whether their wives kept flocks
of " them congested ducks." They
knew exactly what they wanted, land;
and they saw in the Board, whose
intentions were so plainly beneficent,

a means by which land might be got. By
a process of silent pressure they gradually
diverted the Board's energy from diffuse
philanthropy and got it concentrated on
the business of buying and reselling land
in parcels of convenient size. The Board,
moulded into shape by the intelligence of
the class for which it set out to play providence, became at last an independent and
unco-ordinated part of the machinery
established for the transference of the
ownership of the Irish soil from the landlord to the tenant. In only one important
particular does the work of the Board
differ from that which the Estates Commissioners are doing for the rest of Ireland.
The Congested Districts Board builds
houses for its clients. They are exceedingly
ugly houses and have done as much as any
work of man can do to spoil the charm of
the Irish landscape. And they are not
popular. The people would very much
rather have built their own houses. But
even an Irish farmer cannot get all he
wants in this world exactly as he wants it,

and the possession of land in sufficient quantity was the main thing. It is a small matter, when you have got the land, that you have to live in a house that you do not like, planned and built by some one who does not know that it is convenient to be near water when clothes have to be washed, who thinks that the top of a shelterless hill is a suitable place for human habitation in a land swept by the gales of the Atlantic Ocean.

Having got what he wanted by political action, the Irish farmer has shown himself capable of making good use of his opportunities. The magic of property has proved a stimulus to exertion. Everywhere in Ireland the standard of comfort has risen and is still rising among the farmers. They are making their houses more comfortable. They are furnishing them better. They are planting fruit trees, are developing a taste for flower gardens, are learning to grow, use and appreciate vegetables unknown in rural Ireland twenty-five years ago except in the gardens of the rich. And they are devoting intelligence to their own proper business of farming. Labour-saving devices, often co-operatively owned, are becoming more and more common. The value of milk records, as guides in the weeding out of unprofitable cows from herds, is getting to be understood. Faced by the emergency of the food shortage during the latter part of the war the Irish farmer showed himself capable of a rapid change in his method of farming. He tilled, and tilled successfully, where he had been accustomed to graze. Not even the panic-stricken meddling of officials, caged in city offices, threw the Irish farmer out of his stride. When the regulations made for his guidance were transparently idiotic he managed to ignore them. He supplied food, saved the country from a total lack of milk and butter, and kept his head while prices, controlled or uncontrolled, bounded about like balls on an uneven tennis court.

In the management of local public business the farmer has made wise use of the powers that came into his hands at the

passing of the Local Government Act.
The County and District Councils of rural
Ireland occasionally make themselves
ridiculous by passing flamboyant resolutions. But resolutions are well understood
in Ireland, and the passing of them is
recognised as a harmless way of placating
troublesome enthusiasts. When it comes
to things which matter, the rates for instance which must be paid, the farmers
and their representatives are strictly busi-
nesslike. Urban and city corporations are
sometimes wildly extravagant, sometimes
grossly careless, in their use of public
money. The farmer realises that public
money is his own money, since in the end
he has to supply a good deal of it, and his
fault is not extravagance. He is even
inclined to be penurious, scrutinising expenditure on public work too minutely and
paring down the salaries of his servants.
If we compare the emoluments of the
officials of the Dublin Corporation with
the incomes allotted in rural Ireland to
dispensary doctors we understand why the

rates in Irish cities are sometimes very high and in rural districts surprisingly low.

Niggardliness in private life is generally reckoned the besetting sin of the peasant proprietor and of the small yeomen class. The Irish farmer seems to be escaping it. He has not yet learnt to give money, though he will give almost anything else ; and charitable institutions, if they are to be dependent in the future on the generosity of the farmers, are likely to suffer. But the farmer is learning to spend. The money he has made through his ability and energy in meeting the emergency of the war is not being entirely hoarded. The accounts of the great drapery companies show largely increased expenditure by some sections of the community on women's clothes, and often on women's clothes of the finer kind. It is the farmers' wives who are buying. Jewellers and silversmiths, though the expenditure of their old patrons has been severely curtailed, yet find that their business is increasing, It is, they say, the farmers who

are buying. At country auctions articles
of furniture of fine and valuable kinds are
eagerly bought by farmers. So are pianos,
mechanical piano players, and even pictures. The demand for such things shows
not only a willingness to spend money
freely, but an intelligent desire for a more
cultured and fully developed life than that
lived by farmers in the past.

We have been assured, by newspapers
and public speakers, that there has been
an orgy of extravagant expenditure in
England, and that certain classes, suddenly
possessed of considerable sums of money,
have been reckless and foolish in their
buying. The munition worker's fur coat
has passed into a kind of proverb. This
may be so in England, or the statements
made may be merely another example of
the curious fables which pass for facts in
times of excitement. There is certainly
no wild extravagance among Irish farmers.
There has been and is free expenditure,
but it has been, on the whole, reasonable,
and is certainly justified by the position of

those who spend. Some time ago at an unimportant country auction an oil painting was offered for sale. The auctioneer could give no account of it and there was no way of discovering the artist's name. There were present at the auction two men who might be supposed to know something about art. They bid against each other for the picture, and no one else seemed interested in the sale until the price rose to £30. At that point a farmer joined in the bidding and finally secured the picture, offering more than either of the original competitors. In speaking of the purchase afterwards he said that he wanted a picture to hang on the wall of his parlour. He wanted a good picture, a picture by a real artist. He felt convinced that what he had bought must be a good picture, for otherwise Mr. A. and Mr. B., his competitors at the auction would not have tried to buy it.

The incident is exceptional, perhaps singular, but the story is a very good illustration of three things—the farmer's ability to buy, his reasoned cautiousness in buying, and his appreciation of the fact that there are certain desirable things to be bought about which he ought not to trust his own judgment.

Will the Irish farmer be able to retain the power and keep or improve the position he has gained ?   As owner, or prospective owner, of land, the one solid, irremovable thing, he seems secure.   As a skilful and intelligent master of an indispensable business, the production of food, he is in a very strong position.   As a hard worker—and he does work hard—he escapes the reproach of living on the fruits of other men's labour, a reproach which in the modern world weakens the position of the idle capitalist. He has considerable political power, and in an Irish Parliament—if such a thing ever comes into existence—would have more power than men of any other class.   But he is threatened.   His property and the profits he has made out of it are looked at enviously by the agricultural labourer, and in Ireland the agricultural labourer is efficiently organised, well led, and not in the least afraid to strike. The farmer's political sagacity and his class solidarity won him his victory over the landlords. Will he prove as able in defence as he was in attack ? Repeated demands have lately been made by the labourers for increased wages and shorter hours of work. Hitherto the farmer has been content to compromise. Under the present conditions he can afford to pay almost any wages and still be sure of a substantial profit. But the present conditions are abnormal. Very soon the farmer will have to face the competition of foreign countries sending their produce to the hungry markets of Great Britain. There will be a limit to the possible profits of farming, a limit enforced by competition against which no tariff barriers are likely to be an efficient protection.

Then the farmer will have to fight it out with the labourer, and the labourer is sure of a great deal of public sympathy. His organisation is no trade union limited to men of his own profession. It is part of a union which includes most of the poorer labourers of the cities. He will have them at his back in his struggle against the farmer, very much as the farmer had the support of the town shopkeepers and minor professional men in his struggle against the landlords. And there will be a general feeling that it will do the farmers no harm to be bullied a little. They have done well for themselves and they have not cared much what happened to any one else. There is always a certain joy, an unholy joy, in seeing an engineer " hoist with his own petard." And the tactics with which the labourer will fight the farmer are likely to be very much the same as those with which the farmer fought the landlords.

The struggle will be a particularly interesting one for the dispassionate and detached observer to watch—if indeed there is in Ireland such a thing as a dispassionate and detached observer. For the matter at issue between the farmer and the labourer is purely economic. It is scarcely possible for either one side or the other to confuse the issue and embitter tempers by an appeal to religion. Behind the obvious economics of the agrarian struggle there was always the feeling that the landlords represented a Protestant aristocracy, the farmers a Catholic democracy. The politics of the Home Rule and Union contest were white hot because religion, or what in Ireland goes by the name of religion, inflamed the combatants. But there is no discernible difference between the religion of the farmer and that of the labourer. In Ireland, though we have fought each other for centuries, we have never yet fought without the inspiration of our own particular kind of religion. If we do so now it will be a new thing in our history and therefore of extreme interest. But it is rash to prophesy that such a purely secular controversy will take place. Perhaps—though it seems impossible—we shall drag religion into the business somehow. Perhaps, lacking the religious impulse, we shall in the end decline to fight at all.

After all a fight for wages and hours of work, indeed any fight, is a poor thing, unsatisfying to the spiritual nature of man, when you cannot denounce your opponent as a bigot in this world or cherish a comforting belief that he will have a hot time of it in the next.

CHAPTER IX

THE MIDDLE CLASSES—DUBLIN

IF I were compelled to live in a city—
from which fate may Heaven defend me!
—I should choose Dublin rather than any
other I have known. This is the judgment
of mature years, arrived at slowly, after
some experience. I began with a strong
prejudice against Dublin. I went there
first when I was eighteen years of age, and
I was sure then that it was wholly contemptible. It was, so I believed, a place
where people talked a great deal, for the
most part very foolishly, where people did
very little, because they were lazy and
hated work. It was therefore a place
which could not be rich and prosperous.
Nothing useful was made there. No ships,
no linen, no rope. It was, besides, a city

with pretensions, posing as the capital of
the country ; whereas Ireland, then for a
long time happily made one with England,
had no capital of its own. London seemed
to me to be our capital, just as London is
the capital of his country to a Yorkshire-
man, though Leeds and Sheffield are important towns. Dublin scarcely seemed to
me even important.

I do not remember that any one ever
taught me these things or said them to me
in plain words. I was born and brought
up in Belfast. There is no need to tell a
Belfast boy things like those about Dublin.
I breathed them in with the air of County
Antrim. I absorbed them through the
pores of my skin in Donegall Place.

Arriving in Dublin at Amiens Street
Station, as all strangers from the north do
and must, I added to my prejudices a
distinct impression. Dublin was shabby.
Belfast does not give the stranger this
impression however he arrives there. The
Belfast terminus of the Great Northern
Railway stands in a wide thoroughfare,

and the buildings which the traveller sees first are ugly, perhaps, but not shabby. York Street Station is set in a large space redeemed by mere size from shabbiness. The County Down Railway disgorges its passengers near the riverside and the clamour of Harland and Wolff's shipbuilding yard is in their ears. There is nothing worn out or shabby about Harland and Wolff's shipbuilding yard. But the surroundings of Amiens Street Station are very shabby. I drove, I suppose, across the swivel bridge and through Tara Street. I passed close to the Custom House indeed, but too close. It is not possible to see a building when you are just underneath it. And all that corner of Dublin was even shabbier then than it is now

Nothing that I have seen of Dublin since has altered that first impression. It is vividly renewed every time I visit the city after a sojourn elsewhere. I once spent some weeks in New York, and when I came back the shabbiness of Dublin was a shock to me. After London I feel it acutely.

And it is not simply a matter of comparison with other cities, newer perhaps, or richer. I got the same impression when I walked the streets of Dublin after months spent among the stony fields of Mayo, than which no places I have ever seen look older and poorer. I get it now when I go to Dublin from the pleasant pastures of Kildare.

But my opinion of shabbiness has changed. It used to seem to me merely contemptible; as a pair of boots, never stretched on trees, much wrinkled and patched, seems contemptible to a well-dressed woman. I know now that there is something to be said for old boots, even if they are so old that they let in a little water on wet days. There is a sense of ease in wearing them. They press no corn. They have adapted themselves to ill-shaped toe joints, and after all there are few of us—few at all events who have reached even middle age—whose toe joints are not distorted a little. And it is not only Tara Street and the swivel bridge, or

Baggot Street and St. Stephen's Green, and glorious Grafton Street itself, all of them in their way very shabby, which suggest old boots. The life of the city has the same quality. No man's feet are pinched in Dublin. No man's corns need trouble him. There is a tolerance, an easiness, a sense of general forbearance.

Perhaps shabbiness and good-humour are necessarily connected so that we cannot have the one without the other. Dublin might very well be cleaner than it is, and smarter, more punctual in its business ways, more exact, more prompt. But if it were, it would almost certainly be less pleasant to live in. Did any one ever know a woman who kept her house spotless and shining who did not also keep her family somewhat in terror of her sharp tongue and her temper? Dublin may be a slattern. It cannot be said of her that she is a shrew.

As it is with my first impression of Dublin's shabbiness, so it is with my still earlier prejudices. They were fairly right about the facts. They were all wrong in

their estimate of values. Dublin is, for
instance, inordinately fond of talking, and
this is specially true of intellectual Dublin.
St. Luke—if indeed St. Luke wrote the
Acts of the Apostles—noted that the
Athenians spent their time in nothing else
but either to tell or to hear some new
thing. Dublin even preserves the Athenian
order, putting telling first and hearing
second. It desires to tell, that is to talk,
and only consents to hear because life is
necessarily an affair of give and take.
Unless a man occasionally listens to other
people he cannot expect other people to
listen to him. Yet Dublin's capacity for
listening is admirable and very wonderful
considering that it has to listen to the same
things over and over again. For Dublin
has improved upon Athens and its way of
living. It is by no means necessary in
Dublin that the thing told should be new.
Indeed if the talking of intellectual Dublin
were limited in subject to new things there
would be much less of it than there is.
There are not nearly enough new ideas in

the world to furnish forth the intellectual feasts of all Dublin's clever men. They, very wisely, use old ideas, making " great argument about them and about."

Dublin is naturally, instinctively, hospitable. Nowhere else, not even in New York, are strangers better treated. They are dined and wined, feasted and fêted day after day. And Dublin hospitality is as spontaneous as it is generous. A stranger there is not a burden laid on his entertainers, but a prize to be snatched at and even scrambled for, because a stranger is willing to listen. Indeed he must listen, for he is very seldom allowed to talk. I remember a dinner-party given in honour of an Englishman of great eminence, a man who ranks among the very first of our contemporary writers. He did not, I think, make one remark during the whole meal. But he heard, perhaps with interest, many things very well said. At such a dinner given elsewhere the other guests would have sat round and waited for the lion to roar—and this was a veritable lion.

There, the lion's mouth was closed, as tightly as if Daniel had been in the den with him. The others did the roaring. And this, I daresay, was very good for the lion.

The abundance and excellence of Dublin's talk are in sharp contrast with the very moderate amount of Dublin's accomplishment. The city contains a large number of thinkers who have worked out theories of government and are prepared to expound to audiences of any kind how Ireland ought to be governed, or England, or Russia, or any other country. But they have not succeeded in actually governing Dublin in any tolerable way. There are men in Dublin, not only in public offices where they might be expected, but in all sorts of odd places, who know exactly how commercial and business success is to be attained, who will teach the farmer how to farm, the banker how to bank, every one everywhere in Ireland how to become prosperous and rich. But they remain quite poor themselves. There are critics

233

of literature in Dublin of extraordinary acuteness and delicacy of feeling who will talk about "tendencies" and "notes" and "movements" for hours at a time until the brain of the plain man swims, until he grovels admiring and abased before the feet of those who know so much and talk so well. But Dublin produces very few books which any one can read.

I remember talking to a man, a citizen of Dublin, about the number of brilliant intellectuals who captivate strangers when they visit our shores. I mentioned, with all due reverence and sincere admiration, the names of some of the deepest thinkers in Ireland.

"Before I settle a man's reputation," said my friend acidly, "I like to see him succeed in a competitive profession. None of these fellows ever do."

The Belfast man in me assented cordially. Another part of me, a nobler part I trust, revolted against the judgment. Success in a competitive profession is not the only success or the best. The pursuit of an idea—even if you never catch the elusive thing—is a nobler sport than the pursuit of material wealth. We may perhaps compare the life of intellectual Dublin to the activities of an enthusiastic entomologist on a summer day. Equipped with a green gauze net he chases butterflies about a garden, bright winged insects which shine pleasantly in the sunlight and rival the flowers themselves in colour. In the same garden there is a man who digs. His shoulders are bent. His eyes are on the dull brown earth. In the end, if he perseveres, that man will have potatoes to eat, good satisfying stuff which will fill his belly. But the entomologist, if he succeeds, will have a butterfly, stretched out and pinned down on a board, labelled and classified, a lasting addition, I suppose, to human knowledge. He will have made a step forward on the long road of science. Even if he fails—and fluttering ideas are very difficult to catch—his will be the glory of having tried. Besides, chasing butterflies is far pleasanter than digging.

But not even an entomologist is wholly indifferent to bread and butter, and Dublin, though it does not want to make a fortune, does want, if possible, to be paid a salary. Elsewhere men will toil early and late, struggle, strive, deny themselves and imperil their immortal souls in the hope of establishing great businesses, seeing bank balances grow, piling up gilt-edged securities, building in the end huge gaunt mansions in bare fields and giving orders to Maple & Co. to furnish them regardless of expense. In Dublin this kind of ambition is extremely rare. Success in Dublin, the success which is valued and sought, is not measured in accumulated property, but in the size of a salary, paid quarterly or half-yearly from a secure source. And success is not the prize of ceaseless toil. It is the fruit of influence, wisely used.

In the suburbs of London there are men who live comfortably in villas of moderate size. Every morning at a fixed hour they

disappear from their houses and do not
return again till the evening. Their neighbours, even their wives, do not know
where they go or what they do. In speaking of one of them we say : " Oh, So-and-
so is something in the City." The description is vague but sufficient. We know that
the man is engaged in business of some sort,
selling carpets perhaps, or discounting
bills. He is—so the phrase goes—" making
money." In Dublin there are men living
in a similar way in similar villas, who also
leave their houses for some hours every
day, and their neighbours do not know
exactly where they go or what they do.
In speaking of them we say : " Oh, So-
and-so is something in the Four Courts,"
or " He has a job in the Castle." Again
the description, though vague, is sufficient.
We know that the man is serving the State
in an office. He is drawing a salary.

Dublin is a fortunate place for those who
prefer earning salaries to the chance of
making fortunes. It is the seat of the
Government of the country, a Government

which does not indeed possess the power of governing, but, while all or almost all else has been lost, retains its power of patronage. Dublin Castle cannot make laws or even enforce those which are made elsewhere, but it can appoint secretaries and clerks—and pay them. I am sometimes inclined to think that the " Irish Question," that despair of philosophers, historians, and statesmen, might, so far as middle-class Dublin is concerned, be boiled down to a struggle for the power of patronage. Given a community in which the highest ambition of most men is a well-salaried post, and you get a society which is intensely, even passionately, concerned about the power of patronage.

Patronage is important everywhere, but far more important in Dublin than in most other places. The number of salaried posts there is very great in proportion to the population. A few years ago some one wrote a pamphlet about the Government Boards in Ireland and called them " The Forty Thieves." His wit betrayed him

into an exaggeration and an understate-
ment. Our public offices are not so dis-
honest as to deserve the name of thieves.
That is the exaggeration. There must be
far more than forty of them. That is
where the author, with the Arabian Nights
fresh in his mind, understated his case.

Dublin is also the centre of the legal
system in Ireland, and the greatest prizes
in the lottery of salaries fall to lawyers.
It is better to be a judge than the head of
a State Department. Even a county
court judge has a very comfortable
position. And there are all sorts of offices,
more or less well paid, which lawyers get
as a matter of course, often as a matter of
professional right. A man of great ability
may prefer to earn a very large income as
a lawyer by his own exertion. Two or
three men in every generation aim at and
achieve this kind of success. But for most
lawyers success means securing a salaried
post, something in which a fixed amount of
work is done, during a fixed number of
hours, for a fixed salary.

Outside Government circles and the legal profession the same kind of ambition prevails everywhere in Dublin. The Corporation provides salaried posts. The Poor Law Guardians provide salaried posts. Friendly societies—now heavily subsidised by the Government—provide salaried posts. And everybody wants such posts. A girl, applying for the position of sewing maid, described herself in a letter as " compelled by family misfortune to try and make an honest living." The man who through lack of family connections or political influence cannot hope for a salaried post is in the position of that girl. He may make things, bicycles or motor-cars. He may sell stocks or shares, or cure the sick, but, if he is a true Dubliner, he feels that he has been unjustly treated by fate in being compelled to make a living instead of having one provided for him by a benevolent providence.

All this helps to make Dublin a very pleasant place to live in. Elsewhere the successful man is often most offensive.

He is inclined to be arrogant and self-assertive. It is by his own industry, his own ability, and his own daring that he has succeeded. He cannot help saying so on every possible occasion, and a society in which people say such things is not nice to live in. The beauty of most success in Dublin is that, like the Order of the Garter, there is no damned merit about it. The successful man knows this and does not boast. His manners remain suave and friendly. He can be hospitable without embittering the souls of his guests by pointing to his great possessions, without saying—by look if not by word—" There, my boy, you might be drinking wine like that every night, or sitting opposite that genuine Sheraton sideboard, if you had worked as hard all your life as I have."

The successful Dublin man neither says nor thinks such things. He owes his well-salaried security to the fact that his wife's uncle had influence somewhere. There is nothing to boast about in that. It might have been somebody else's wife's uncle who had the influence, or the other political party might have been in power at the time. The chess player will rejoice and may swagger when he wins. He who throws dice successfully will rejoice but not swagger.

There are, of course, great manufacturing and commercial companies inDublin. There is Guinness's Brewery for instance, and the Bank of Ireland. But they remain of subordinate importance and are affected in their methods by the spirit of the city. A clerkship in Guinness's is not regarded as an opportunity for commercial energy or enterprise. It is like the " something in the Castle," a provision for life, a salaried post from which a man starts on no adventures after fortune, but at which he rests in security, looking for increments of pay as the years flow softly by. A clerkship in the Bank of Ireland is, I am told, slightly less desirable than a clerkship in the Brewery. But it is essentially the same kind of thing. Both fall to those who have influence, whose friends know some one who knows some one else, who is in a position to ask for a nomination with some prospect of securing it.

I do not wish to discuss the abstract question of the wisdom of this method of appointment by influence. I know that a strong case can be made against it, that the voices of honest reformers are loud in wrath when they denounce it.

It is no doubt an abuse, but like many abuses it has certain practical advantages. The great thing, of course, is to have influence, but that is necessarily the happy position of very few, of a small minority even in a city like Dublin where there is an immense amount of influence going. Next to having influence oneself the best thing is to be on terms of friendship with those who have it. " To quarrel with your bread and butter " is recognised as foolish all the world over. In a society where influence is, if not almighty, certainly very powerful it is just as foolish to quarrel with those who are able to provide your bread and butter, or the bread and butter of your son, or the bread and butter of your daughter's husband. There are some people so highly placed that they plainly possess great influence. Every one is friendly with them. But quite obscure, apparently insignificant people sometimes have influence too. It is never possible to say even of a lonely old maid that she has no influence. The wise man keeps on good terms with every one, quarrels with no one if he can possibly help it. Since wisdom is, after all, far commoner in the world than folly, a society in which it is foolish to quarrel with any one becomes a very pleasant society to live in. In Dublin friendliness has become a habit; and life is easier, smoother, far less irritating there than in other parts of the United Kingdom. Thus does the abuse of advancement by interest and influence yet wear a precious jewel in its head. Who will say that the evil of the system outweighs the good? Who will hurry to perpetrate an unnecessary and certainly unpopular reform?

The friendliness which is characteristic of Dublin does not exist only among the classes which earn salaries and inhabit suburban houses. It prevails in all classes and, a more striking thing, between all classes. Indeed class distinctions seem to matter less in Dublin than they do elsewhere. There is a hymn which I have heard sung in England. One of the verses runs thus :

> "The rich man in his castle,
> The poor man at his gate,
> God made them high and lowly
> And ordered their estate."

That hymn was written by an Irishwoman, but I never heard it sung in Ireland. I cannot imagine it sung in a Dublin church with any appearance of solemnity. Dublin does not look at life in that way. The English do. They may like that view of things or they may hate it. They are probably happier when they like it ; better men when they hate it. But neither by liking it nor hating it do they get away from it. They accept the fact that God ordered their estate such as it is. They may think He did wisely, or they may think He did wrong. But it is a solemn fact that He did. Dublin does not think so.

There are, no doubt, in Dublin men who have the appearance of being rich, and a good many who are undoubtedly poor. But there is no recognition of an impassable gulf between the two. God made them both men and women. The hawker who calls with a basket full of fish is friendly, and spends a pleasant twenty minutes discussing the effect of the Vartry water upon children's teeth. In England he would be conscious that some superior divinity had ordered his estate. He would touch his hat, name his price, deposit a herring, and go. He might as well be a penny in the slot machine for all the interest he takes in his customer or suffers his customer to take in him. The Dublin tram conductor—when he gets away from the congestion of Nelson's Pillar somewhere at the end of a long line—does not merely puncture tickets for a passenger. He gives his views, sound sensible views, on the misleading nature of the headlines printed in the evening papers. An English tram conductor, angrily conscious that God had ordered his estate, would maintain his attitude of tram-conducting if he and his passenger were marooned together on a desert island without hope or prospect of getting away for years.

Dublin—the fact strikes every visitor—is singularly infested with beggars. In New York there are no beggars. In London it is only after dark and in lonely streets that anybody begs. They say that begging is an illegal practice, and that the police in London, New York, Paris and elsewhere, put a stop to it by arresting the beggars. But that is not the real reason for the decay of mendicancy everywhere except in Dublin and Oporto. There are police enough in Dublin to arrest every beggar in the city in less than a week. Man for man the police are far more than a match, physically, for the beggars, who are indeed mostly women and children. Begging must be just as much against the law in Dublin as anywhere else. If it were a matter of police and law there would be no beggars in Dublin. But neither the law nor the police are nearly as important as they look. Dublin has found that out and Dublin does not want its beggars arrested. The law may say what it likes and the police may grow to any height, but if a city wants beggars it will have them. And Dublin does. It is part of the prevailing friendliness of the place.

It is not possible to do business in Dublin without being struck by the fact that even commercial life is deeply affected by this same spirit of friendliness. Dublin there is no use denying the fact—has not a high reputation in the business world. Talk to a Belfast business man about Dublin and hear his opinion. If he is a very kindly Belfast man he will say that Dublin is incurably slack. But what is the matter with Dublin as a business city is not slackness but friendliness, that tolerant

" live and let live " spirit which oils the
wheels of affairs so that they run smoothly
even if they do not run very fast.

There is a story told by Miss Somerville
and Miss Ross about a man who started
a fish shop in a small south of Ireland town.
He went out of business almost at once
because people kept bothering the life out
of him for fish. His philosophy was not
that of a commercially-minded business
man. He wanted, not to make a fortune,
but to live quietly. He would have been
willing to supply fish in moderate quantities to a few people once a week or so.
He saw no sense in becoming a slave to a
clamorous population which demanded fish
in unreasonable quantities. Dublin shares
his feeling. Business is business of course,
an unpleasant necessity for many people.
But it is foolish to run into extremes.

There are a certain number of people
who want to take houses in Dublin every
year, and Dublin is abundantly supplied
with house agents. Every one of them is
an agreeable and friendly man. They have

long printed lists of possible habitations
on which the number of rooms, acres of
land, rental and other details are plainly
set forth. The aspiring tenant takes the
list and sets out to view the houses. He
goes at some expense of time and money
to Howth and searches out a house which
seems as if it ought to be the thing he
wants. He is met at the door by a smiling
parlourmaid, who tells him that it was,
she believes, to be let once, but was taken
on a long lease six months ago. Still
hopeful the searcher goes to Rathfarnham
and finds another house. It is indubitably
to be let. There are bills to that effect
in the windows. But there is no possible
way of getting inside it. The key is,
perhaps, somewhere. Perhaps there is no
key. The stranger from England or Belfast goes back to the house agent, after
five or six of these experiments, in a furious
temper and complains that his time has
been wasted. The house agent is perfectly
agreeable and friendly.

" Do you tell me that now ? " he says,

when he hears that the house at Howth has been let. "Maybe then I'd better scratch it off the list."

But he does not scratch it off. After all it may be vacant again some day. And if it ever is trouble will be saved by having it on the list.

Faced with the fact that the house at Rathfarnham is inaccessible he expresses astonishment.

"Well now," he says, "aren't some people the very devil? You'll hardly believe it, but it was only yesterday the owner of that house was asking me was there any chance of getting it let. And how is a gentleman to take a house if he can't see the inside of it? Tell me that."

The stranger of course cannot tell him that. He is asking the same question himself. But his bad temper is oozing away. He is beginning to realise that business in Dublin is a matter of give and take. A house agent must not be pinned down to the printed statements of his lists. It is unfriendly to treat him in that way. As for the loss of time! Man has an immortal soul. All eternity lies before him. It is a supremely silly thing to fuss about a day or two.

There ought to be a statue of Epictetus somewhere in Dublin. It is his philosophy which rules. He enumerates, I recollect, certain troubles which make fools angry, and he exhorts his disciples to bear them quietly. "For so much peace is bought," he says. "This is the price of tranquillity." Such is the Dublin spirit. It makes no fetish of efficiency. Man does not live in order to get things done. He is forced to get things done, more or less, in order to live. If he can succeed in living comfortably and peacefully without getting much done or troubling a great deal in the doing, then he has mastered destiny and achieved the highest wisdom. Dublin is far advanced towards this beatitude.

The friendliness of Dublin is something more than mere good-humour. It is the result of a deep philosophy, of a wide and tolerant outlook upon life. Very few things, perhaps no things at all, are really important enough to worry about. Ireland is—I quote popularly accepted opinion—the most religious country in the world, and Dublin is the capital of Ireland. Yet Dublin is, broadly speaking, a city of sceptics. I am far from suggesting that there is any considerable number of people in Dublin who express out loud doubts about the chief articles of the Christian creed. I am sure that the proportion of Dublin people who go to church regularly is unusually large. Yet Dublin's attitude towards most things is that of a detached, slightly amused spectator. Dublin is very rarely stirred to enthusiasm about anything. No doubt this scepticism is to some extent due to the fact that the city is full of officials. An official cannot be a fanatic. He must not take sides or feel anything very strongly. The perfect official, if such a thing existed, would believe nothing firmly except that most men are fools. Dublin's officials have undoubtedly modified the

Dublin spirit. But I do not think that the whole credit for the sceptical sanity of Dublin can be given to the official class. Trinity College has had its influence. There are people who affect to regard Trinity as an alien institution. But it has succeeded in inspiring Dublin with some of its own spirit. Trinity lives upon Butler's Analogy. There are, I believe, some men with Trinity degrees who have not studied Butler. But they have not therefore escaped his spirit. Trinity is soaked in him. Nowhere else in the world has that great book, the perfect expression of pure common sense, been so highly honoured as in Trinity. " Probability," says Butler, " is the very guide of life." Precisely. Trinity lives and Dublin, with the Trinity influence continually modifying it, also lives with probability for guide. But certainty is the source of all en-thusiasm, all fanaticism, all passion. No man raves or wants to slay his fellow-man for the sake of a greater or less degree of probability. Nothing less than a certainty will make him either a persecutor or a martyr. Friendliness, detachment, sanity, these are the rewards of a life guided by probability, the fruits of the Butler spirit.

Dublin reached the zenith of its career as a city at the end of the eighteenth century. It is to that period or thereabouts that its most beautiful buildings belong. Since then the world has progressed, so they say, or gone mad. There is a cartoon by Max Beerbohm which shows " the grave misgivings of the nineteenth century and the wicked amusement of the eighteenth in watching the progress (or whatever it is) of the twentieth." The eighteenth century in the picture is represented by a beau, appropriately dressed, in the act of taking a pinch of snuff. Every line of his lean face expresses a cynical appreciation of the extreme folly of the twentieth century, who is rushing along with his motor goggles pushed back on his forehead. I am far from suggesting that Dublin is as cynical as that old gentleman. It is much too kindly to be cynical. Nor is Dublin's amusement at the world's progress in the least wicked. But Dublin watches the progress (or whatever it is) with a certain detachment. The motor cyclist, bent double and heralded on his way by a series of rapid explosions, speeds by. Dublin looks at him and wonders where he wants to get to; doubts whether it is worth while getting there at all; is almost certain—Dublin is never quite certain—that there is no use getting there so quickly.

CHAPTER X

THE MIDDLE CLASSES—BELFAST

BELFAST has the largest flax spinning mill in the world, the largest rope works, the largest tobacco factory, the largest shipbuilding yard, and, I daresay, several other largest things. She contributes, through her Custom House, more to the Imperial Treasury than any other city in Ireland. I am not sure—statistics never stay long in my head—that she does not pay more in this way than all the rest of Ireland put together. She is progressive, far more progressive than Dublin or Cork, cleaner, better lighted and—much, much else. All these facts—if they are facts, I may have got some of them wrong—are impressive, especially when conveyed to the world in shouts. They would be even more impressive if they were shouted by anybody except Belfast herself.

It is always wiser for a man, a city, or a nation to get an outsider to act as trumpeter. He who sounds his own praises seldom gets the credit which is his due. That goes to the man or community which sits still, smirks modestly and blushes, if possible, while somebody else, not a near relation, sings "the glorious day's renown." Perhaps Belfast is too honest for such a trick. Perhaps there has been a difficulty in getting a disinterested stranger to say what ought to be said about Belfast. So Belfast says it herself, all of it, several times over, very loud.

Yet we ought not to allow this little failure in modesty, this trifling aggressiveness of manner, to blind us to the fact that what Belfast says about herself is true. The York Street spinning mill really is very large. So is Gallaher's tobacco factory. Harland and Wolff's men did build the *Titanic*. Belfast does possess a fierce kind of energy in work which is not to be found elsewhere in Ireland.

I paid a visit a few days ago to the little apiary in which I keep a hive or two of bees. I had, a few days before, housed a great swarm in their new home. I found them intensely, feverishly busy. There were no drones among them, for drones are not wanted in these new communities. Each worker was possessed with a very demon of energy. Not for one instant did the returning adventurer linger on the alighting board. No clusters hung, sunning themselves on the porch. I could hear the restless hum of the workers inside, desperately intent on forming wax cells. Near at hand was another hive, the home of the parent community from which the swarm came forth. I knew that inside it there were great combs, well stored with honey, heavy with maturing brood. Here the workers went in and out quietly, gathered in groups round the porch and enjoyed the sun. Great drones, glossy, well-favoured fellows, went buzzing to and fro. Life was a leisurely business. Summer days were long. The world was a pleasant place. Why seek an early grave by unremitting toil ? We can scarcely suppose that each bee reasons and acts as an individual, convinced of the necessity for breathless work, or of the pleasantness of leisure. Rather it seems as if there were a kind of community spirit which possesses the society, against which the individual bee is powerless. The members of the newly-hived swarm must work, must wear themselves out with working, dare not pause for an instant. The community spirit compels them. Belfast, a city of restless energy, is a newly-hived swarm.

Visitors to Belfast complain that people walk too fast along the streets, that the greetings of passing friends are of the briefest, and nods of recognition curt. The Belfast man takes such criticisms as compliments, tributes paid unwillingly to the spirit of his city. " In Dublin," he says, —Dublin is always the antithesis of Belfast— " men walk about, up and down Grafton

Street, as if they wanted to air their clothes. When we walk along Donegall Place it is because we want to get to the other end of it, and the sooner the better, for we've something to do." Then perhaps he mentions the size of the York Street spinning mill and the number of riveters that work in the shipyards, and adds—for the matter is seldom far from his thoughts—that Belfast will not be governed by a Dublin Parliament. He is perfectly right. In Belfast people do walk as if they wanted to get there, and I doubt whether a Dublin Parliament will ever govern Belfast. It seems much more likely that Belfast will bully a Dublin Parliament, if there ever is a Dublin Parliament; but curiously enough, the Belfast man does not think so.

I had occasion once to travel from a midland town to Belfast by way of Dublin. I arrived at the Dublin terminus of my first railway and beckoned to a porter. He smiled pleasantly at me and then suggested to another porter that he should undertake the task of carrying my luggage. The second porter did it with the air of a man of abundant leisure, who out of the kindness of his heart assists a fellow in distress. I daresay I did not look as if I were good for much in the way of a tip. Yet I had ready in my pocket a modest coin which I gave apologetically to the second porter. Later on I arrived in Belfast. I had not bought a fur-lined overcoat or a new hat on the way. I looked neither more nor less opulent than when I reached Dublin. A discerning porter with a knowledge of travellers must have been able to gauge to a halfpenny the size of the tip I should give. Yet long before the train stopped a Belfast porter was running alongside the carriage in which I was, eager to carry my luggage. Unfortunately for him, there was another porter, equally eager and much stronger. Just as the train stopped he reached the first porter and struck him a heavy blow on the chest. While the stricken man reeled back, this second porter secured my belongings and in the end pocketed my tip. This story, though true, is a parable.

Belfast is pervaded by a spirit of intense and serious earnestness. Dublin is more suave. I do not mean that the Dublin man when he makes a speech in public is any less terrific than the Belfast man. Both thunder, and no one living can do more than that. But when the Dublin man has finished his speech he relaxes. The Belfast man goes on thundering in private life. At midnight, when the meeting is over and the cheering done, your Dublin orator will even smile over his pipe. The humorous side of his own enthusiasm is quite visible to him. The Belfast orator does not know that there is a humorous side to enthusiasm. No quantity of tobacco will lure him off the platform. I should not be surprised to hear that he continues in a condition of deadly earnestness even after he has gone to bed. Far be it from me to argue about the comparative moral worth of intermittent and perennial earnestness. I think I admire the Belfast kind more, but the Dublin kind is pleasanter to live with. Yet if any one disagrees with me about this I give in to him at once. I will not quarrel about the point. What interests me far more than the value of either earnestness is the question about how there comes to be this difference between the two cities. They are very little more than a hundred miles apart, yet I suppose that Manchester and Bombay are not more separated in spirit.

Difference of race is, I suppose, part of the explanation we seek. It is, at all events, often insisted on, and there seems to be some reality in it. The Belfast man is near akin to the Lowland Scot. There is, and for centuries has been, much going to and fro between Scotland and this part of Ireland, and much intermingling of Scottish and Irish blood. But it is very easy to exaggerate the importance of race in determining character, at all events in Ireland. Neither in Belfast nor anywhere else in Ireland do we find racial

Babylon that I have built ? " Then, so
we read, his heart was lifted up within
him. He felt the call to do still greater
things. He did not do them, it seems,
because God, Who will not let men build
their towers right up to Heaven, drove him
forth to eat grass in the fields like an ox.
But the energy, the breathless desire of
effort, were in him stimulated by the
sight of all that he had done. Men who
find less to do because more has been
done for them by those who went before
are not so forced into ambitious effort.

Belfast can scarcely escape the Nebu-
chadnezzar spirit. It is plain and well
within the memory of the middle-aged
that this is the great city which we have
built. It is not so long ago since old St.
Ann's, the Presbyterian church in Fisher-
wick Place and the Linen Hall were the
most impressive buildings in the city ;
since the stretch of land between the
Botanic Gardens and the Ormeau Road was
" the Plains," a barren, uninhabited tract ;
since the Black Staff flowed visible and

evil-smelling under bridges; since the wayfarer passed straight into the country when he left the Queen's College behind him, and St. John's, Malone, a tiny church, stood among fields where cattle grazed. In less than the passing of a single generation the old buildings have disappeared. A cathedral rises where St. Ann's stood. The sordid slums behind it have become orderly rows of warehouses. A great municipal building has taken the place of the modestly respectable Linen Hall. "The Plains" are thickly-populated streets. The houses of prosperous business men stand one beside the other, in the middle of trim grounds, out to Shaw's Bridge. Living men have seen the foundation stones laid, have watched the walls grow, the streets widen, the tentacles of traffic routes stretch and extend their grasp. A sense of restlessness exists when rapid change challenges the attention, and restlessness is readily transmutable into energy.

The beekeeper knows that his swarm, newly hived, will work deliriously because it has everything to do, because it is new, is at its beginnings. He knows that it will go on working even after it has accomplished much, will cover fresh combs with brood and store crates full of honey beyond its needs, because the spirit of work has possessed it, because the sight of all it has done drives it on to do still more.

Whatever may be the causes of the energy of Belfast, there can be no question of its value. There is a story—probably quite untrue—told about an English statesman who was questioned about Ireland at a time when the war was passing through one of its critical stages. " I don't care," he said, or is supposed to have said, " if the whole of the rest of Ireland is swallowed up by the sea so long as Belfast is left to build ships and make linen." If the singular energy and force of Belfast were, as the story suggests, of vital importance to the Empire and to England, it is not difficult to understand that Ireland would be poor without this wayward northern city of hers. England and the Empire have energy and force in abundance. Ireland—the Ireland outside the Belfast sphere of influence—lacks just this capacity for savage toil.

And Ireland is instinctively conscious of her need. The southern Nationalist, even the southern Unionist, often speak harshly and angrily about Belfast. The Nationalist at least is not without excuse. Belfast—it may almost be said Belfast alone—has stood between him and his hopes; and this is very hard to forgive. Belfast has the defects of her fine qualities, is arrogant, and contemptuous of much that she does not understand. Belfast, with blunt rudeness, refuses to discuss or to reason. She states her will aggressively, provocatively. It is scarcely to be expected that Belfast should be much loved. It would not be surprising if the rest of Ireland, in a fit of petulance, were to disown Belfast and bid her go her own way, make her own bed and lie in it. But Ireland has never yielded to such a temptation. She claims Belfast as part of her body and will listen to no scheme of settlement which lops off the northern limb of the nation. In this the rest of Ireland has shown herself as obstinate as Belfast herself.

There are, no doubt, many reasons which make the idea of partition hateful to Ireland. If Ireland is to be a nation at all she must preserve her geographical unity. She is an island. Within the bounds of her four seas there are no natural divisions. No range of mountains, no river system, cuts her in two. There is no separation of highlands and lowlands. Any division of Irish soil would be artificial and the boundaries would correspond to no geographical facts. It is possible to conceive two politically divided States in Scotland. In that country there might be a nation or two nations. In Ireland there is no such alternative. There may be a nation or there may be a couple of provinces. There cannot be a nation and a province, or a nation with an English county cut out of it. If Ireland is to have national existence of any real kind, Belfast must be part of Ireland.

There is the feeling that to desert the Nationalists of Belfast, to leave the minority there helpless under the rule of the majority, would be a betrayal. Belfast has the same feeling about the Unionists of the south and west of Ireland; but Belfast, narrowly self-centred, does not shrink from the sacrifice as the rest of Ireland does. She is prepared, unwillingly indeed and as a last resort, to leave the friends of the Union elsewhere in Ireland to their fate, a fate so evil, according to her belief, as to be intolerable. Nationalist Ireland thinks otherwise and will not leave her friends to the tender mercies of Belfast.

But behind the reasoned Nationalism and the party loyalty lies the sense, instinctive and trustworthy, that Ireland cannot afford to do without Belfast; not only because Belfast is a source of financial strength, a very taxable city, but because Belfast possesses certain qualities, energy, the spirit of commercial adventure, hardness, which the rest of Ireland lacks. It is for the sake of these that Ireland, wise at heart even when she seems fanatical, will not let Belfast break away from her.

Belfast has not yet understood that she cannot do without Ireland. Convinced that she possesses the great qualities which she does possess, she supposes that these are sufficient. They are not. The experiment of Free Cities, denationalised centres of pure commerce, was tried in Europe, and the cities failed to survive. Napoleon found some of them impossible. Those which survived his conquests were gradually drawn into unions, Zollvereins, empires. They could not continue their independent existence because there is something stronger than the cash nexus and the bonds of credit. Man does not live by bread alone, even though the bread be won abundantly by building ships and making linen. One by one the Free Cities of eighteenth century Europe felt the drawing of the spirit of nationality and became one with their kin. Belfast can no more stand apart from Ireland than Hamburg could stand apart from Germany. Something greater than politics, deeper than creeds, decides these things in the end. Men and communities cannot in the long run successfully defy the law of Him Who made them what they are and placed them where they are.

CHAPTER XI

THE MIDDLE CLASSES—THE COUNTRY TOWN

It was about three o'clock in the afternoon. I met the Resident Magistrate in the street. He had left the Court House and was on his way home to luncheon. I knew him for a kindly, easy-tempered man, usually cheerful. That day he was not cheerful. He had scarcely a smile for me, though we were good friends.

There were several excuses for a ruffled temper. The Court where his work lay had sat for an unusually long time and he was no doubt hungry. The day was very wet and the streets of the town were in a condition of indescribable filth. There had been a fair the day before, and the smell of it still lingered, rising in a vapour which could be seen as well as smelt, from the slime which the fair had left. The soft warm rain encouraged the smell and kept the filth liquid. My friend was one of those men who take a pleasure in being well-dressed. He hated splashing his trousers with evil mud, trousers which he regarded with pride and affection. That was another excuse for ill-temper.

But I knew him well enough to give him credit for a buoyancy of spirit sufficient to float him off the shoals of depression in spite of hunger, wet and mud. I greeted him and began to feel about sympathetically for the cause of his mood.

" Troublesome Court to-day ? " I asked.

Petty Sessions Courts in Irish country towns are not very troublesome as a rule. The casual drunkard is easily dealt with. Cases of assault and wilful trespass are often quite amusing, and no magistrate of any experience allows himself to be perplexed by the curiously contradictory evidence of reputable and thoroughly credible witnesses. He gets at the truth without troubling himself overmuch about sworn statements. But sometimes Petty Sessions Courts are very troublesome, and a magistrate has to be careful what he says and does. When offences of political or semi-political complexion are considered a lawyer is often brought down from Dublin, met at the station with a band, well fee'd and well fed. His business, in return for welcome, food and fee, is to harry the Resident Magistrate as much as he can. He does this thoroughly and with skill. But there had been no such case in the Court that day. If there had been I should have seen the crowds in the streets and heard the cheering and the band.

"Licensing sessions to-day," said my friend the magistrate.

Licensing sessions are held once a year and are of enormous importance. They are, in the commercial life of an Irish country town, the most important events there are. At them it is decided which shops are to have the privilege of selling porter and whisky. It is a very valuable privilege, for the sale of porter and whisky is the surest way, indeed almost the only way, of making money in an Irish country town.

"We did well to-day, anyhow," the magistrate went on. "We licensed every house in the whole damned place, except mine and the Rectory. I told them they might as well make a clean job of it and license them too."

The statement was a gross exaggeration, excusable only in a man who had been much tried. I looked up and down the long street. I could see three drapers' shops and a watchmaker's, which were none of them licensed and were not likely to be. There were also several labourers' cottages, built by the Urban District Council, in which nothing was sold. There were the houses of two doctors and——I did not mean to argue with my friend, or to press my instances of unlicensed houses on him. He would not have listened to me if I had.

"Look at this town," he said. "What

is there in it ? A church, a great huge church, two churches in fact, both far too big. Both built out of the profits of selling drink. What else ? An enormous staring workhouse, bigger even than the churches, filled with the people who bought the drink. Beautiful, isn't it ? The way things work in with each other. Drink damns the people's souls and destroys their bodies, so drink erects churches to save the souls and workhouses to keep the bodies alive. Come home and have lunch with me."

I did, and we each had a whisky and soda. After that we felt better and my friend was able to talk calmly. We agreed that common report, and he himself following it, had wronged the Irish people. They do not in fact drink more than any one else. There are comparatively few habitual and hopeless drunkards. Our country towns are, indeed, so full of public-houses that their number strikes the most unobservant stranger very unpleasantly. But there are fewer inns and drinking places along the country roads than there are in England. The drink traffic in Ireland is centralised and the drinking is all done on market days and fair days. The Irish farmer or farm labourer has his drink when he comes into the town, once a week for a market, once a month for a fair. On the other days he does not drink at all. The numerous public-houses of the country town, which stand side by side the whole length of the street, are busy once a week and very busy once a month. All the rest of their time they are almost empty. The grotesque statement about the workhouses and the churches is simply not true. There are all sorts of people in workhouses and workhouse hospitals besides broken drunkards, and churches are not built entirely out of whisky money. If ecclesiastics succeed in skimming the cream off the drink traffic by way of subscriptions, dues and " dowries " of nuns, is not this a victory for religion and morality ? If the devil has no right, as Wesley thought, to the best tunes, it is surely meritorious

to despoil him also of his other gains ; even
granting that whisky is the devil, which
has never been absolutely proved.

The problem of the public-houses which
fill the streets of Irish country towns is,
in reality, more economic than either
religious or moral. A town, even an Irish
town, ought to be something more than a
distributing centre. It can scarcely justify
its existence or expect to exist very long
if it only distributes, or mainly distributes,
drink. Yet this is the position to which
our smaller towns are rapidly sinking. A
hundred years ago they were centres of
productive industry. They have now
almost ceased to produce. Railway facili-
ties, the enterprise of large advertising
firms, and the growth of co-operative
societies are undermining their position
even as distributing centres of most kinds
of goods. If the farmer can buy his seeds
better from a co-operative society, and
the farmer's wife can buy her dairy
requisites cheaper in Dublin, and the
farmer's daughter can obtain a wider

choice of blouses and stays by writing to
Manchester for a price list, the shops of
the small towns will be left with nothing
which can be sold profitably except whisky
and porter. The future seems far from
hopeful. The workhouses will soon become
the real centres of the town's life. The
churches will perhaps grow larger. The
public-houses can scarcely be more numerous than they are. An intolerable dullness,
like mildew, will settle on these places,
and the grass growing in the streets will
be the freshest and pleasantest thing about
them, unless ——

Once these towns were productive. I
came across evidence of this fact quite
accidentally. I was sitting one winter
afternoon in the housekeeper's room of a
" great house " which dominated and had
owned a small country town. I was having
tea with the housekeeper, an old lady whose
charming manners made me think better
of the " Bladesover System " than Mr.
Wells does. We were friends before that
afternoon, the housekeeper and I. We

became confidential and intimate over our tea. Afterwards she opened for me some large store cupboards and showed me an immense hoard of linen. Some of it was nearly a hundred years old. So she assured me, and added :

" You couldn't buy linen like that now, whatever you paid for it."

I fingered the venerable fabric. It was still sound and strong.

" It was made here," she told me. " The flax was grown here and the linen made here, in the town."

I was astonished. Linen, so I had always supposed, is the peculiar treasure of Belfast, one of the chief sources of that great city's wealth. Could it be that this decayed, shabby, and remote little town had ever challenged Belfast and made linen ? I remembered an old spinning wheel in a cottage, unlike the wheels on which women in those days spun their balls of grey wool. An old, old woman, the owner of the wheel, told me that her mother had used it for spinning linen thread from flax. I remembered a kind of arcade in the town, used when I knew it as a housing place for vehicles, which had once been known as the linen market. The town had certainly, at one time, made linen.

The fact set me searching, wandering through those unexciting pages of history which do not record battles or remote antiquities, but the domestic doings of our great-grandfathers. I found out about that town that it was once, not a hundred years ago, a hive of most varied industrial life It had a distillery, a large affair which made 60,000 gallons of whisky in the year. It had two breweries, two salt works (whatever salt works are), and a tannery. It had two flour mills worked by water wheels of thirty horse power, two cotton mills and a bleach green, as well as its linen manufactory and market. It imported immense quantities of flax seed and timber from America and the Baltic. It exported grain, flour, and meal. Of all these industries not a single

284

one remained. One of the breweries was the last survivor and it perished some years ago ; killed, I think, by legislation made in the interests of temperance. It was probably legislation which killed the whisky distillery too, causing a thirsty people to obtain their 60,000 gallons of whisky elsewhere, from some company large and rich enough to survive the blows of Acts of Parliament.

For the failure of the cotton factories, the linen making, the salt works and the tannery we should not, I suppose, blame the malignant jealousy of an alien Parliament ; though we do blame it, for our own comfort and satisfaction. These industries perished because, under modern conditions, such work must be done on a large scale ; and factories have gathered into great centres. That town might, perhaps, have become the great centre of linen manufacturing. It did not. Belfast beat it in the race.

Is there any hope for the future of these small Irish towns ? Will they ever again justify their existence by producing things ?

Of late years many efforts have been been made to start industries here and there. Sometimes a precarious existence is secured for a woollen mill or a bacon-curing establishment. But there is always a feeling that any promise of real success would be the signal for some of the long-established and mighty competitors of the new industry to rise and slay it. Often no slaying is required. The infant struggles a little, cries plaintively, and then dies quietly. There are several reasons for such failure. Ireland is not rich in coal. The people of our small country towns have lost the industrial habit. But chiefly, I suppose, we must blame the fact that nobody really believes in these new industries. Capital is subscribed, scantily, by patriotic and philanthropic people who do not look for and therefore do not get a return for their money. The workers have a dim belief that their wages will be paid by some one, probably a Government

Board, whether the industry succeeds or fails. Nobody who merely wants to make money ever dreams of starting any kind of factory in an Irish country town. And, unfortunately, success in industry is a prize reserved only for those who want to make money and want to make it very much. Patriots and philanthropists look for—will no doubt get—other rewards.

I have heard it argued that the industries of our Irish towns might be re-established by a system of protection and bounty, such as would perhaps commend itself to an Irish Parliament independent enough and powerful enough to control the country's fiscal policy. The thing is, no doubt, theoretically possible. The industrial success of Germany seems to have been fostered by tariffs, the German economist List is as great a favourite with Irish Nationalists as Karl Marx is with English Socialists. But an Irish Parliament with the power of imposing tariffs at will seems a long way off, and even if it existed it is very doubtful whether it would be of use to our smaller towns. As long as the conditions which destroyed their industries continue the most rigid and wisely considered system of tariffs could do nothing but increase the industrial efficiency of our few great towns. The small towns lost their industries because the growth of the factory system centralised manufacture. Protection against English competition might re-establish certain industries in Ireland, cotton spinning, for instance, and tanning. There is no reason to suppose that it would re-establish them in the small towns which lost them, not through free trade, or any other legislative changes, but through the pressure of economic conditions which made it necessary to work in large centres and destroyed the life of small factories.

All that can be said is that the present system of industrial organisation is not eternal and already shows signs of giving way to some other system. A few mechanical inventions and the recognition of the power of coal made the nineteenth century factory system inevitable. A few more inventions and the development of the power of electricity may make the factory system impossible, and substitute for our present great centres of specialised production a number of small factories scattered over the country. Such a change would give our Irish country towns a chance of regaining their lost position as centres of production as well as distribution.

Meanwhile our Irish country towns are not only poverty-stricken, they are for the most part incurably ugly. A small English town, one of those which have escaped the prosperity of the industrial revival, may be sleepy and half dead; but very often it has a singular charm. There is an air of brooding peacefulness about it. The eye rests with content on the pitch of the roofs of the houses, their timbered fronts, their dormer windows. The square-towered church seems to be soaked with the lives of quiet-living people. The market square is spacious. The main street delights us with its picturesque irregularities. I suppose that these English towns have suffered during the nineteenth century much as small towns have in Ireland. But in England the town has retained its self-respect. It is an old maid, a little prim, far past her prime, unfruitful; but gentle, sweet, and decked with delicate old fineries. The Irish country town is a woman who has lost her self-respect, has become a slattern with draggled petticoats and boots with gaping holes in them. The older buildings in these towns have neither beauty nor dignity; but at least they escape being offensive. The newer buildings—churches and convents are almost the only new buildings in these Irish towns —are, as a rule, not only undistinguished. They have a positive quality of ugliness. There are exceptions, of course, new churches here and there which are as good as any one is likely to build anywhere; but the traveller passes through many towns before his eyes are gladdened by the sight of one of them. It used to be the fashion some years ago to blame the Roman Catholic Church for spending too much money on ecclesiastical buildings. " To what purpose," said the critic, quoting Judas Iscariot, " to what purpose is this waste ? " The complaint was unfair. A Church ought to spend money freely to the glory of God, and, from the Church's point of view, money is better spent on cathedrals than on drains. But very ugly churches are not a glory to God, and the more money that is spent on them the more the angels must feel inclined to weep. That, however, is a matter to be settled between the ecclesiastical authorities and the angels. The outsider has no right to meddle in the controversy—if indeed there is a controversy, a matter about which we cannot feel sure, for angels may actually like ugly churches.

The point of the ordinary Irishman's complaint, one on which he may fairly claim to be heard, is the effect of the erection of very ugly buildings on the life of the people of our towns. The spiritual development of men and women must be checked if they grow up among old buildings which are sordid and new buildings which are both pretentious and vulgar.

Life in these towns is very much what we might expect, grey and a little bleak. They are forcing hotbeds of the worst kinds of snobbishness. If Milton were alive to-day and were engaged now in writing " Paradise Lost " he might be tempted to depose Mammon from his position as " Least erect of spirits that fell," and put Snobbishness in his place. Mammon, base as he is, at least demands some fine qualities from his worshippers, perseverance for instance, and capacity for toil, without which the smiles of the money god can scarcely be won. Snobbishness—a fallen angel who once companied with feudal chivalry—is served acceptably only by the mean. In purely country places where class distinctions are very sharply marked snobbishness scarcely exists. In great cities inequalities of wealth create class divisions which at least have the merit of being real. The poor, whatever their pretensions to gentle birth, cannot share the life of the well-to-do, because they cannot afford to live it. The well-to-do, though they may trace their descent right back to Adam, or, better still, may belong to some county family, cannot associate intimately with the very rich, because their incomes do not allow them to keep yachts, polo ponies, and Rolls-Royce motor-cars. But in small Irish towns no obvious inequalities of wealth exist. Every one is equally poor—most people indeed are equally in debt—except the successful money-lending shopkeeper, and he makes no display of his wealth. Nor are social distinctions clearly and naturally marked as in the country, where the lord of the manor belongs to one class, the farmer to another, and neither of them disputes or wishes to emphasise the fact. In the small town one class shades off into another and there is no rational excuse for social divisions. Yet the divisions exist, as acute as they are unreasonable. Men and women, of equal wealth, of similar education, with identical tastes, indistinguishable in culture and manners, firmly and decisively refuse to associate with each other on no grounds whatever except that a clerk in a bank and his wife " do not know " a clerk in a land agent's office ; while the clerk in the land agent's office '' does not know " a shop assistant, even though the latter asserts his quality by calling himself " a young gentleman in a business house."

The existence of this spirit of snobbishness would be deplorable if it did no more than spoil the social life of our towns, making it duller and greyer than it need be. Unfortunately, owing to the peculiar conditions of Irish life snobbishness adds an unnecessary bitterness to every one of the real divisions which exist among us. It is a deplorable fact that it is, socially, rather more " respectable " to be a Unionist than to be a Nationalist, because the landed gentry are for the most part Unionists. It is slightly more " respectable " to be a Constitutional Nationalist than a Sinn Féiner, because the wealthier Nationalists are not enthusiastic about an Irish Republic. In the same way a curious aroma of social superiority clings to the profession of the Protestantism of the Church of Ireland, because, I suppose, most of the gentry who used to be " landed " are members of that Church. Irishmen of different religions and different political views get on very well together if they happen to belong, unmistakably, to the same class. They do not at all events quarrel oftener or dislike each other more than men of different religions and different politics in other countries. What creates the singular bitterness which marks our Irish religious and political differences, what does more than almost anything else to make the Irish question the insoluble conundrum it has become, is the unfortunate fact that class divisions to some extent run along the lines of political and religious cleavage; and seem to do so more than they actually do. It is com-

AN IRISHMAN LOOKS AT HIS WORLD

paratively easy to forgive a man for being
a Roman Catholic or for being a Protestant.
It is not actually impossible for a Nationalist to recognise the honesty and patriotism
of a Unionist. What is extraordinarily
difficult is to see any good in a man
who claims social superiority for no con-
ceivable reason, or threatens to intrude
into the sacred circle of social exclusive-
ness.

Next to its snobbishness the worst
feature of life in small Irish towns is the
prevailing intellectual apathy. Carnegie
Libraries, though plentiful, have done very
little to create an interest in books or their
writers. I have heard it maintained by a
man who rather prided himself on his
general intellectual superiority that Mrs.
Humphry Ward wrote the fashion columns
in a popular weekly paper. He was
certain about this, and was even prepared
to bet on it, because his aunt had told him
so. Most of us believed him, and no
actual harm came to any one through the
mistake. But it was evidence of a general

ignorance which was a little startling. I have heard Thackeray mentioned as the author of "The Adventures of an Irish R.M.," though the speaker lived in a town not a hundred miles away from the home of the two ladies who created Major Yates and Flurry Knox.

Pictures are totally unknown, even by reproductions. A stranger, settling in an Irish country town, once hung up some reproductions of Fra Angelico angels in her drawing-room. They were seen there and carefully studied by a lady, one of the social leaders of the place.

"Yes," she said, "I know that kind of church picture is quite fashionable at present, but I don't care for it myself."

Our Irish literary revival has had little or no influence on the life of our country towns. The intellectual interest of the people is politics—if politics can be called intellectual. And even politics are not popular except in the form of speeches, if possible speeches about some event of local interest. A crowd can be gathered on market day in almost any town by an orator who will denounce the conviction of a local cattle driver. The brilliant articles and pamphlets in which Mr. Arthur Griffith outlines his Sinn Féin policy—in days long before speeches were made about Sinn Féin—were read, at most, by half a dozen people in a country town.

I happened to be living near a small town when Mr. Asquith's ill-fated Home Rule Bill was first introduced. The morning papers did not reach that town till noonday. We depended for our earliest parliamentary news on the evening papers of the day before, which came to us by a night train, arriving at 2 a.m. or some such unhallowed hour. I was anxious to learn what Mr. Asquith's plan of Home Rule was. I went into the town immediately after breakfast, arriving there about 9.30 a.m. I hastened to the shop of the principal newsagent.

"Have you got a copy of one of last night's evening papers left?" I asked eagerly.

The man pointed to a pile of papers on his counter.

" You can have as many as you like," he said. " Nobody else wants one."

" Do you mean to say—— ? " I began.

" I ordered two dozen of them papers specially," he said, " on account of that Home Rule Bill that was brought into Parliament yesterday, and I haven't been asked for one this morning except by yourself."

Ireland had been demanding Home Rule, or denouncing Home Rule, with enormous vigour and persistency for upwards of half a century. Yet when a Home Rule Bill was actually introduced into Parliament and seemed likely to pass, the people of that town cared so little about it that no single individual among them wanted to spend a halfpenny on an evening paper to find out what an English Premier, convinced at last of the need of a measure of some kind, intended to do with our country.

Yet this condition of mental apathy is

neither inevitable nor natural to the people of our small towns. I have written in another chapter something about what the Gaelic League did in awakening interest in the Irish language and the history and customs of our country. I have seen other experiments tried on a much smaller scale, which go to show that the people in these towns, in spite of their depressing surroundings and the prevailing snobbishness, are capable of intellectual effort and might find a richer and fuller kind of life than any they have hitherto known.

At present the one redeeming feature in the life of these small towns is the general interest in sport. This alone seems to have the power of obliterating, for a time, at all events, class distinctions, and rousing people from apathy.

CHAPTER XII

CONCLUSION

A WRITER is over-sanguine who expects that his book will be read; but he can comfort himself with the reflection that it will certainly be criticised if he has been fool enough to write about Ireland. He may say with the prophet Isaiah, "I have offered my back to the smiter, my cheeks to them that pluck off the hairs; and not hid my face from shame and spitting."

The plain man, a sane and kindly critic, speaks impatiently. He takes a book, reads a page or two here and there, skipping the pages in between, and then—if the book is about Ireland—demands of the author a plan, a policy, a scheme for the settlement of the Irish question. "It's all very well writing like that," he says,

" and if things weren't in the perfectly beastly state they are I'd read your stuff. But just now—Ireland is a damned nuisance and you Irishmen are—— Why can't you tell me straight in a few words what you want ? If it isn't absolutely insane I'll do it. I'll do anything to keep you quiet for a decade or two." Alas ! I understand the feelings of the plain man. Being a plain man myself, one of the very plainest, I sympathise. If I had, or could compound, a solution of the Irish problem, I should—how gladly !—roll it into a pill, easy to take at bedtime with a glass of water, and present it to the plain man, or to our Ministers of State, or to the American public, or to any one else whose stomach is sick with undigested Ireland.

The earnest reformer speaks to the same effect, but sadly rather than impatiently. He is as solemn as a judge, or, since judges very seldom are solemn, as solemn as a judge's robes. He is oppressed with a sense of the world's great need of constructive thought. He looks at me with sorrowful reproach, as one of the Apostles might have looked at Nero fiddling while Rome burned, though I am not an Emperor and did not set the place on fire. " Is this a time," he says, " for barren talk, when all that is best in Ireland is earnestly engaged in reconstructive effort ? What is your plan ? Where is your answer to the sphinx riddle which we must answer lest we die ? " I feel the justice of the reproach, and if I could construct, or re-construct, or even instruct, I should " for-swear sack, live cleanly," and never smile again.

Indeed I am more interested in Ireland than in anything else and I love every sod of it. But for a solution to the problem, an answer to the riddle, a scheme of settle-ment—I have no such thing to offer. I think that all the solutions, answers, and schemes there are have been proposed already. It is unreasonable to expect me to invent a new one. There can be, we are told, just so many permutations and combinations among any series of figures or letters, so many and no more. There is no use trying to devise an extra one. So with plans for the government of Ireland. There are perhaps two hundred different ways of governing Ireland. They have not all been tried. Indeed, I doubt if any one of them has been tried. But they have all been proposed and recommended. I cannot invent another, because there is no other to be invented. Nor am I so arrogant as to suppose that I can advocate any of them more eloquently and persuasively than its inventor.

And why should I try ? It is the business of statesmen and politicians to arrange constitutions and set them working. That is their job. We pay them to do it. My business is to live, as best I can, under the governments which they devise. I do not attempt to teach the plumber how to plumb or the carpenter how to saw when I hire them to mend my house. They would resent my impertinence if I did such a thing. Why should I teach the politicians how to do their work ?

There are plenty of them and they are all very clever men. Our ancestors were surely right when they made their proverb about the foolishness of keeping a dog and barking oneself.

It is just possible that constitutions and politics and revolutions and constructions and reconstructions matter very much less than we think they do ; and that governments, even if very bad or very good, affect men's lives only slightly. Alexander Pope was of this opinion and expressed it very neatly in one of his carefully constructed lines :

" For forms of government let fools contest."

But Alexander Pope lived a long time ago and his political wisdom is out of date. I am far from suggesting that it is foolish to try to preserve the Union or establish a republic. But we are inclined, in Ireland we are very much inclined, to hold exaggerated views about the importance of constitutions. A man may work hard and speak the truth under almost any form of

government; and a nation is great, even
free, if most of her citizens work hard and
speak the truth. This is, I know, an unpopular doctrine, and any one who preaches
it deserves to be burnt at the stake for
heresy. Yet it is worth considering whether
it is the State that makes the man or men
who make the State. For this is what it
comes to in the end. If it is really true
that we can make good citizens, diligent,
courageous men, by setting up a good
kind of government, then there can be no
nobler occupation than politics, and we are
right to struggle hard to establish—whatever it is we want to establish. For
having got our perfect State we shall
have perfect men in it. But if it is true
that only good men can have a good State,
then the work of the priest and the school-
master is more important than the work
of the politician, professional or amateur,
and the work of the mother and father is
more important still; for these are engaged in making men what they are
and so, in the end, are making the State

what it is. If this is true—and it may be—
then we Irishmen, all of us, are spending
most energy on what matters least, the
form of the State; and far too little
energy on what matters most, the making
of men, that education which goes on con-
tinuously from the cradle to the grave.

PRINTED IN GREAT BRITAIN BY
RICHARD CLAY AND SONS, LIMITED,
BRUNSWICK STREET, STAMFORD STREET, S.E. 1,
AND BUNGAY, SUFFOLK.